Eastern Theater 1861–65

Confederate Cavalryman
VERSUS
Union Cavalryman

Ron Field

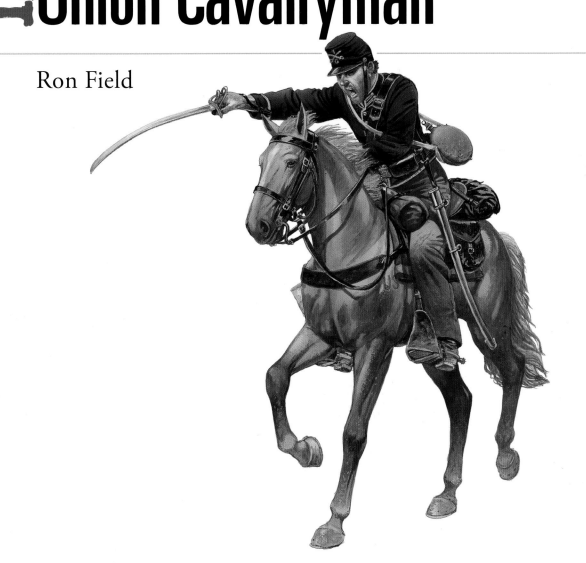

First published in Great Britain in 2015 by Osprey Publishing,
PO Box 883, Oxford, OX1 9PL, UK
PO Box 3985, New York, NY 10185-3985, USA
E-mail: info@ospreypublishing.com

Osprey Publishing, part of Bloomsbury Publishing Plc

A CIP catalog record for this book is available from the British Library

Print ISBN: 978 1 4728 0731 1
PDF ebook ISBN: 978 1 4728 0732 8
ePub ebook ISBN: 978 1 4728 0733 5

Index by Mark Swift
Typeset in Univers, Sabon and Adobe Garamond Pro
Maps by bounford.com
Originated by PDQ Media, Bungay, UK
Printed in China through Worldprint Ltd

15 16 17 18 19   10 9 8 7 6 5 4 3 2 1

Osprey Publishing is supporting the Woodland Trust, the UK's leading
woodland conservation charity, by funding the dedication of trees.

www.ospreypublishing.com

Acknowledgments

A special thanks to Ken R. Knopp for his expert advice on the
Confederate cavalryman, and to Eric Wittenberg for sharing his
knowledge of the Union trooper. Thanks also to Sara Buehler,
Collections Registrar, James A. Michener Art Museum, Doylestown,
Pennsylvania; Peter Harrington, Curator, Anne S.K. Brown Collection,
Providence, Rhode Island; Robert Delap, Department of Rights and
Reproductions, The New-York Historical Society, New York City;
Christopher Morton, Assistant Curator, New York State Military
Museum, Saratoga Springs, New York; Eric N. Blevins, Photographer,
North Carolina Museum of History, Raleigh, North Carolina; Clifton P.
Hyatt, US Army Military History Institute, Carlisle, Pennsylvania;
Joseph P. Eckhardt, Jay Barringer, Dr. Michael Cunningham, Alan
Larsen, Dan Schwab; Kristy Wilson, Greg Mast, and Richard Ferry.

Artist's note

Readers may care to note that the original paintings from which the
artwork plates in this book were prepared are available for private sale. All
reproduction copyright whatsoever is retained by the Publishers. All
inquiries should be addressed to:

Peter Dennis, 'Fieldhead', The Park, Mansfield, Nottinghamshire NG18
2AT, UK, or email magie.h@ntlworld.com

The publishers regret that they can enter into no correspondence upon
this matter.

Editor's note

For ease of comparison please refer to the following conversion table:

1 mile = 1.6km
1yd = 0.9m
1ft = 0.3m
1in = 2.54cm/25.4mm
1 US liquid pint = 0.5 liters
1lb = 0.45kg

Key to military symbols

XXXXX	XXXX	XXX	XX	X	III	II
Army Group	Army	Corps	Division	Brigade	Regiment	Battalion
I	•••	••	•	Infantry	Artillery	Cavalry
Company/Battery	Platoon	Section	Squad			
Airborne	Unit HQ	Air defence	Air Force	Air mobile	Air transportable	Amphibious
Anti-tank	Armour	Air aviation	Bridging	Engineer	Headquarters	Maintenance
Medical	Missile	Mountain	Navy	Nuclear, biological, chemical	Ordnance	Parachute
Reconnaissance	Signal	Supply	Transport movement	Fortress or static	Fortress machine gun (MG)	

Key to unit identification

Unit identifier — Parent unit
Commander
(+) with added elements
(−) less elements

CONTENTS

Introduction

Bugles rang through the autumn air sounding "the March" as the battle-hardened troopers of the 1st North Carolina Cavalry drew their sabers and watched the Union column approaching them near Buckland Mills on October 19, 1863. The North Carolinians started off at only a steady trot so as to keep their "column by fours" intact. After advancing some 50yd, the order was given to gallop and about 100yd later Chief Bugler Henry Litaker drew to one side and sounded "the Charge." Pointing their sabers at the reeling troopers of the 2nd New York Cavalry, the North Carolinians spurred their horses on to "the deadly shock" of close-quarter combat, which resulted in another victory for the Southern horseman. Despite advances in technology and the development of breech-loading carbines which enabled cavalry to fight just as effectively dismounted, the charge was still considered the decisive action of Civil War cavalry.

Horsemanship was a way of life in the South. On average a cavalry volunteer from Virginia, South Carolina, or Texas was considered far superior to his Northern counterpart. Horses were used for individual transportation much more regularly than in the North due to a generally poor road system. Furthermore, a strong Southern militia tradition and requirements for local slave patrols to police plantations and catch runaway slaves led to the development of numerous mounted military companies prior to 1861. Southern society was also more stratified, which made its male population more accustomed to a hierarchy of command and better suited to the martial lifestyle.

In the North, neither Brig Gen Irvin McDowell nor Maj Gen George McClellan

Published in the *Charleston Mercury*, this notice placed by Capt Charles J. Shannon, of Camden, South Carolina, called for volunteers for the Kirkwood Cavalry, one of four companies requisitioned from his state "for the war" by the Confederate government in July 1861. Note that the men were to provide their own horses. (Author's collection)

VOLUNTEERS FOR THE WAR.
CAVALRY,

A REQUISITION HAVING BEEN MADE UPON THE STATE FOR FOUR COMPANIES OF CAVALRY, members to furnish their own horses, and it being difficult to organize such Companies in any one District, persons in different portions of the State who are desirous of co-operating in the formation of one of these Corps, will please address
                                    C. J. SHANNON, jr.,
    July 29   6   c   Camden, S. C.

The public clamor for pictorial news of the Civil War created an enormous demand for eyewitness drawings that could be reproduced as wood engravings in illustrated newspapers. Entitled "The 1st Virginia Cavalry at a halt," this drawing on tan paper in pencil and Chinese white was produced by Alfred R. Waud and a wood engraving based on it was published in *Harper's Weekly* on September 27, 1862. The standard bearer proudly carries a cavalry-sized Army of Northern Virginia battle flag and the well-uniformed troopers are armed with carbines and sabers. (Library of Congress LC-DIG-ppmsca-21554)

understood the proper use of cavalry in warfare in 1861 and relegated it in small units to infantry brigades. This organization fared poorly in the Peninsula Campaign and the Seven Days' Battles of 1862. Although Confederate cavalry was also initially used in a piecemeal fashion as scouts and couriers, by the second year of the war it had been properly organized under Maj Gen J.E.B. Stuart, and seriously outperformed its Union counterpart during raids around McClellan's army providing crucial intelligence concerning the enemy. However, as the war progressed, the North took cavalry more seriously and numerous volunteer cavalry regiments were added to the Army. Although initially reluctant to form a large cavalry force, the Union eventually fielded some 258 mounted regiments and 170 unattached companies for different periods of enlistment throughout the war and its mounted branch of service suffered 10,596 killed and 26,490 wounded during the conflict.

Although mass production and the supply of breech-loading weapons would have a major impact on the performance of the Civil War cavalryman, at the outset cavalry in both armies suffered from a lack of carbines. In December 1861, Brig Gen George Stoneman, Chief of Cavalry in the Army of the Potomac, directed that only ten carbines be issued per company while the remaining troopers carried only pistols and sabers. The individual states attempted to alleviate the problem by purchasing whatever was available on the open market, but quantities available were small. This had a negative effect on the ability of the Union cavalry to fight his Confederate counterpart. However, by the end of 1862 the rate of production of Union carbines had improved and a total of 22,545 of various types were in cavalry service.

Lacking the industrial basis of the North, the Confederacy never achieved uniformity in cavalry arms. Starting in May 1861 with only 735 carbines of various patterns, it made various efforts to produce this valuable cavalry weapon during the next few years. Using machinery captured at Harpers Ferry, the South produced carbines at its principal armory in Richmond, Virginia, from 1861, while during the following year weapons of the Sharps pattern were made at the S.C. Robinson Arms Manufactory in the same city.

The Civil War brought the lance into fashion among volunteer cavalrymen in both armies. Interest in the weapon in the North had been precipitated by a European tour of inspection by Regular Army officers such as Capt (later Maj Gen) George B. McClellan, who was sent to observe the Crimean War (1853–56). In 1861 McClellan requested that the 6th Pennsylvania Cavalry be armed with lances which the regiment used in several successful charges during the next 18 months. The lances were exchanged for carbines in 1863 on the grounds that the lances were unsuitable for cavalry service in the wooded country of the Eastern Theater. Photographed at Falmouth, Virginia, the men of Co. I, 6th Pennsylvania Cavalry rest in the field with their lances stacked. (Library of Congress LC-DIG-ppmsca-34477)

The CS government took over the latter in March 1863 and continued manufacture until the latter half of 1864 when the factory was moved to Tallassee, Alabama, where Enfield-pattern carbines were produced.

With its initial lack of interest in cavalry, the Union's supply of horses was inadequate. As the war progressed the North managed the supply of horses more effectively with its system of centralized horse procurement. Commanders often tried to procure specific breeds for their men with the Morgan being a particular favorite within the Army of the Potomac. Although short-lived, the Cavalry Bureau created in 1863 is noteworthy for what it accomplished. A central remount depot was established at Giesboro Point, near Washington, DC, which was supplied with horses purchased at market and could handle between 10,000 and 16,000 horses at any one time.

The Confederacy was far less successful in its provision of horses. According to the Act of Provisional Congress of the Confederate States, of March 6, 1861, volunteer cavalrymen were required to furnish their own mounts and, early in the war, their horse equipment. A trooper received feed, forage, and 40 cents per day as remuneration with his monthly pay, plus repayment of its value should the horse be killed in action – a value that was soon affected by the badly inflated Confederate currency. For those still using their own equipment by January 1863, the government authorized mustering officers to value this for reimbursement as follows: for "a good, serviceable saddle, $15 to $20; good saddle blanket, $3 to $4; good bridle, $3 to $5; good halter, $2 to $3" (Knopp 2001: 166 n11). Needless to say, this was far below CS contract or arsenal manufacturing costs.

The above measures were adopted during 1861 in the belief that the volunteer would take better care of his own property than a government-issued mount. Unfortunately they quickly had the undesirable effect of severely limiting the effectiveness of the Confederate cavalryman. Ranks were continually depleted by troopers returning home to acquire replacement horses, being granted 20 days to do so. Due to increasing incidence of desertion later in the war, only reliable men were given leave to remount themselves. The unlucky trooper that lost his horse in service through disease, malnutrition or exhaustion, but not killed in action, was effectively rendered useless unless he could find and afford another. If a trooper failed to remount

himself, he was forced to become an infantryman, which was considered by many to be an ignominious fate (Munford 1884–85: 346–48).

Toward the end of the war there were various unsuccessful attempts to address the inadequacies of Confederate horse supply. On January 2, 1865, a bill was proposed which, if passed, would have required that horses ridden by cavalry serving outside their home state should become the property of the Confederate States, and the central government would have taken on the responsibility of procuring horses. Most significantly a cavalry bureau was to be established. Unfortunately, this was too little, too late.

Entitled "A Cavalry Charge," this engraving was published in *Harper's Weekly* on July 5, 1862 and pre-dates any real success the Union cavalry had in the Civil War, although it captures the spirit of what was to come. (Author's collection)

This engraving from the *Illustrated London News* of July 27, 1861, shows Confederate cavalry capturing a lone Union dragoon. The latter is depicted in a European hussar-style jacket, of a style worn by some American volunteer militia cavalry companies in antebellum times and possibly during the first few months of the Civil War. (Author's collection)

The Civil War in Northern Virginia, 1862–64

The cavalry clashes explored in this book took place in Northern Virginia which was considered "the seat" of the Eastern Theater of the Civil War. Following his appointment to command the Army of Virginia, Maj Gen John Pope was completely outwitted by Confederate commanders General Robert E. Lee, Maj Gen Thomas "Stonewall" Jackson, and Maj Gen James Longstreet at Second Bull Run/Manassas (August 28–30, 1862), and during the ensuing rout the inexperienced cavalry under Brig Gen John Buford was tasked with covering the retreat of the shattered Federal army across Bull Run. After the Confederate defeat at Bristoe Station (October 14, 1863), Union cavalry under Brig Gen Hugh Judson Kilpatrick rode into a trap near Buckland Mills set by Maj Gen J.E.B. Stuart and Maj Gen Fitzhugh Lee which resulted in another humiliating retreat subsequently known in the Confederacy as "the Buckland Races." As a result of Lt Gen Jubal Early's raid on Washington, DC in July 1864, Maj Gen Philip Sheridan was sent to "burn" the Shenandoah Valley which eventually resulted in the battle at Tom's Brook, where the ill-equipped Confederate troopers of Brig Gen Thomas Rosser and Brig Gen Lunsford Lomax were overwhelmed and routed by the cavalry of the Army of the Shenandoah. What became known in Union ranks as "the Woodstock Races" was considered revenge for what occurred during the previous year. Each of these encounters illustrates how the Civil War cavalryman adapted to a revolution in repeating firearms while continuing to show great courage in the face of more traditional combat.

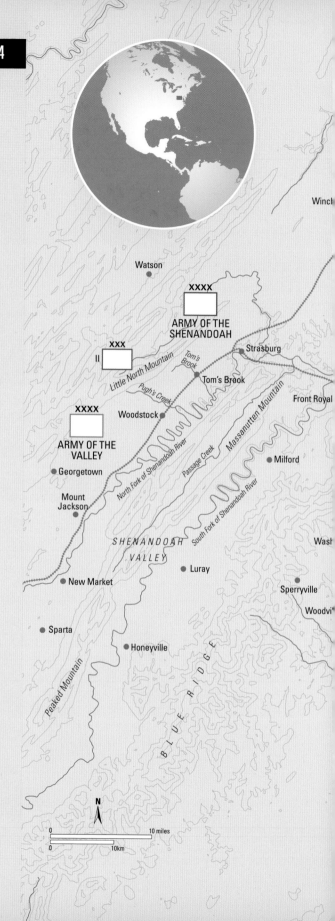

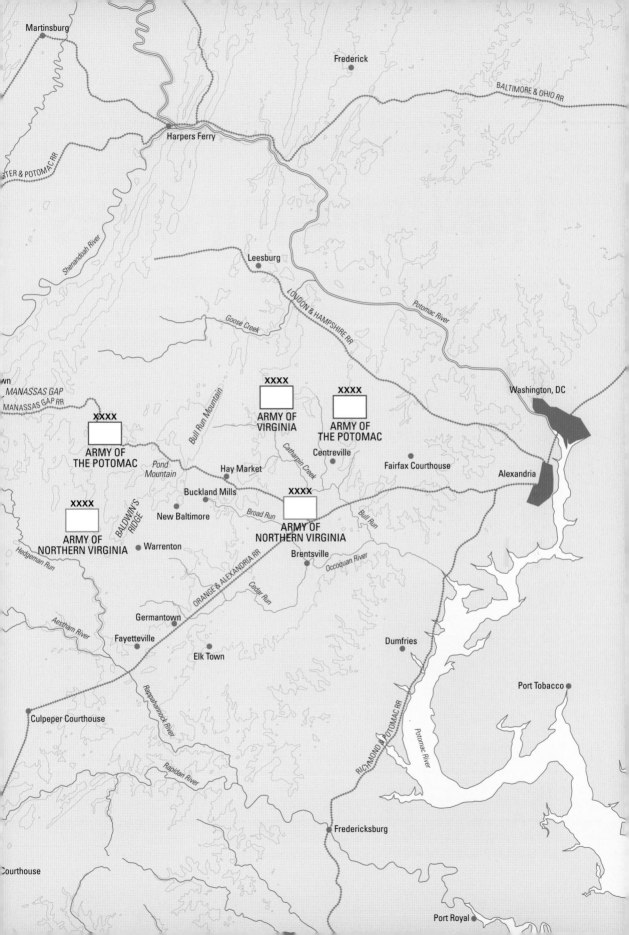

The Opposing Sides

RECRUITMENT AND ORGANIZATION

Union

The first official Union appeal for volunteer cavalry occurred on May 3, 1861, when US President Abraham Lincoln issued a proclamation asking for 42,034 volunteers to serve for "a period of three years unless sooner discharged, and to be mustered into service as infantry and cavalry" (*NYCA* May 4, 1861: 1:2). Although the organization of a few regiments such as the 1st New York, or Lincoln Cavalry, was already under way, it was only after defeat at First Bull Run/Manassas that the Northern authorities began to look with greater favor on the expansion of cavalry. Efforts to raise a regiment of Vermont cavalry began in September 1861 when Lemuel B. Pratt, a wealthy farmer in Colchester, Chittenden County, was issued a commission and instructed to have the unit "ready as soon as possible" (*SADM* Sep 12, 1861: 1:5). Reported to "understand horses and men," and knowing "what kind are wanted for both," Pratt soon recruited the ranks to overflowing in all ten companies of what became the first full regiment of cavalry raised in New England.

Holding the distinction of sustaining the highest battle casualties of any Union cavalry regiment in service, having suffered 174 officers and men killed and wounded, the 1st Maine Cavalry was organized for three years' service in Augusta, Maine, on October 31, 1861. Recruited at Pawtucket, Rhode Island, from December 1861 through March 1862, and the original idea of Governor William Sprague, the "First New England Regiment of Cavalry" contained two battalions of Rhode Islanders, and one of New Hampshire troopers.

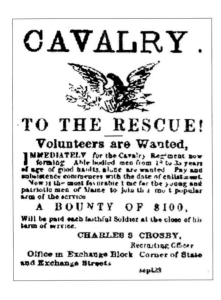

By June 1863, the 2nd Massachusetts Cavalry was offering three-year volunteers $25 when mustered in, and $75 when the regiment left the state (*LDCN* Jun 5, 1863: 2:3). Those enlisting in the 13th New York Cavalry during the following month were promised a Federal Bounty of $402 and a State Bounty of $150 which, with $13 advanced pay, amounted to a grand total of $565 (*NYDR* Jul 24, 1863: 3:5). This system encouraged "bounty jumpers" to volunteer and desert to join another regiment once money had been received.

When first organized, some volunteer cavalry regiments based their structure on that of the Regular Army, which had 12 companies, with two companies in a squadron, two squadrons in a battalion and three battalions in a regiment. However, these battalions were not permitted to function separately as in the Regular Army, and were not allowed extra field and staff. Other regiments had only ten companies organized into five squadrons. Hence, a Union volunteer cavalry regiment might consist of from 1,000 to 1,200 officers and men. Northern cavalry was not normally brigaded until 1863, when they were formed from four to six regiments. In April 1863 Maj Gen Joseph Hooker organized three previously unrelated cavalry divisions into a single corps of cavalry.

The regimental staff of a cavalry regiment consisted of colonel, lieutenant colonel, two or three majors, adjutant (with the rank of lieutenant), surgeon, assistant surgeon, chaplain, regimental quartermaster, regimental commissary of subsistence, and battalion or squadron quartermaster (the last three also holding the rank of lieutenant). The regimental non-commissioned officers consisted of sergeant major, chief bugler (ranked as a sergeant), veterinary surgeon, regimental quartermaster sergeant, regimental commissary sergeant, hospital steward, saddler sergeant, sergeant farrier, and, in some regiments, an ordnance sergeant. A regiment consisted of ten or 12 companies, each of which was composed of a captain, first lieutenant, second lieutenant, one first sergeant, one quartermaster sergeant, one commissary sergeant, five sergeants, eight corporals, two buglers, and a farrier or blacksmith, plus 78 privates. A company was divided into two platoons and each platoon was divided into

Exotic uniforms were worn by some cavalry companies at the outset of the Civil War. This man was possibly a member of a Federal militia company called the Black Hussars. He wears a bearskin cap with bag and plume ornamentation plus skull and cross-bones insignia. His heavily braided coatee has a light-colored aiguillette across the chest. The baldric device consisting of a lion's head and shield on his shoulder belt, and sabertache, or flat pouch, with skull-and-crossbones device plus three stars held in his hand, possibly indicates he was an *aide-de-camp*. An M1840 Heavy Cavalry saber rests across his leg. (Author's collection)

two sections. Each section was further divided into "sets of four." Within some regiments, companies also contained saddlers, farriers, and wagoners. As the war continued the number of troopers fit for duty in a Union cavalry regiment was much reduced due to sickness, battle casualties, and men being detailed for special duties, or as their mounts became unfit for service or were killed in action.

Confederate

At the outset of the war the Confederate government authorized an army that included cavalry as one of its three main branches of service. As a result, numerous mounted volunteer militia companies organized and recruited additional members into their ranks in order to volunteer for state service as individual units. Musicians were much sought after and a rare commodity. On September 7, 1861, the 2nd North Carolina Cavalry (19th Regiment North Carolina Troops) advertised in the *Raleigh Register* for its full complement of "22 Buglers" while at Camp Clark, Kittrell's Springs, in Greenville County. The militia units were supplemented by newly organized volunteer companies. In South Carolina, "Patriotic Young Men" were invited to enlist in the Dixie Rangers for "Twelve Months Confederate Service" on February 14, 1862 (*CDC* Feb 15, 1862: 2:6). By 1863 this unit was Co. B, 5th South Carolina Cavalry. Bounties were also offered Confederate troopers. In order to fill the ranks of his "fine company of Dragoons" for service in the 3rd Georgia Cavalry during April 1862, Capt O.S. Ragland offered "Fifty Dollars Bounty" (*CDE* Apr 5, 1862: 2:4). Commanding the Kirkwood Cavalry, of Camden, South Carolina, Capt C.J. Shannon also promised a $50 bounty provided the men volunteered for two years (*CM* Feb 26, 1862: 2:6). Recruiting notices continued to appear in the Southern press throughout 1862. Enlisting in Co. H, 12th Virginia Cavalry, on August 10, 1862, Pvt James Knox Polk Ritchie recalled the cavalry recruiting song which was also a favorite of J.E.B. Stuart: "If you want to smell hell, If you want to have fun, If you want to catch the devil, Jine the cavalry" (quoted in Frye 1988: 3.)

The size and structure of a Confederate cavalry regiment was smaller in terms of both officers and men than its Union counterpart. This was determined by an "Act for the establishment and organization of the Army of the Confederate States of America," dated March 6, 1861 (*OR* I, IV, 1: 128). The field and staff consisted of one colonel, one lieutenant colonel, one major, one adjutant, one sergeant major, and one quartermaster sergeant. There were ten companies or squadrons each of which was composed of one captain, one first lieutenant, two second lieutenants, five sergeants, four corporals, one farrier, one blacksmith, two buglers, and from 60 to 80 privates. Thus, the official strength of a Confederate cavalry regiment, including field and staff, was about 900 men, although unofficially this was often less. Company strength also varied considerably. For example, at its inception in June 1862, the 12th Virginia Cavalry consisted of a total of 646 troopers with 104 men in Co. A compared with only 42 men in Co. H (Frye 1998: 2). A Confederate cavalry division might have up to six brigades. The number of regiments in each brigade varied from two to six, depending on the strength of the units.

Wastage of manpower was high and as the war went on regiments became steadily smaller. After 1863, they seldom numbered more than 350 troopers. At any time during the war, after an active campaign, it was not uncommon to find regiments down to less than 100 men present for duty. After the war, a former private in the 5th Virginia Cavalry (consolidated), George J. Hundley, recalled, "Our cavalry commands were sadly wasted, regiments being no more than companies and brigades hardly good regiments" (Hundley 1895: 307).

An unidentified South Carolina cavalryman wears a palmetto insignia attached to the band on his 1839-pattern cap. The braid on his gray frock coat is painted yellow in line with the cavalry branch of service. He holds an M1850 foot officer's sword in metal scabbard. (Courtesy of Richard Ferry)

UNIFORMS, EQUIPMENT, AND WEAPONS

Union

The Union cavalryman was usually issued both full and fatigue dress. Originally adopted via General Orders No. 13 on August 15, 1855, for the two regular cavalry regiments then in existence, and prescribed for every branch of the Army in 1858, full-dress headgear for all ranks by 1861 consisted of a dress hat, in post-war years called the "Jeff Davis" or "Hardee" hat. Headwear for fatigue service introduced in 1858 consisted of a forage cap which was essentially of the high-crowned "chasseur" pattern. The popular 1854-pattern "uniform jacket" was worn for full dress and sometimes for fatigue or service duty. Liberally trimmed with yellow braid, this had a high standing collar decorated either side with two false button holes, and was fitted with brass shoulder scales. Fastened by a single row of 12 small cavalry buttons, it had two further buttons on each cuff. Musicians wore yellow "herringbone" trim on the chests of their jackets. The four-button 1857-pattern sack coat was also used for fatigue purposes. White cotton stable-frocks were issued for barracks wear.

The same trousers were worn for dress and fatigue purposes. Made from sky-blue cloth, and usually with "frog pockets" in the front with two-sided openings formed by buttoned flaps, trousers were reinforced with a double thickness of cloth on the seat and inner leg to prolong wear in the saddle. Footwear consisted

Shown here are six single-shot breech-loading carbines used by Civil War cavalrymen. The M1859 Sharps carbine (**1**) with either disc primer or percussion cap was 37.5in in overall length, weighed 8lb, fired a .52-caliber conical ball, and had a maximum range of about 300yd. The M1860 Burnside carbine (**2**) was 40in in length, weighed 7lb, and fired a .52-caliber conical ball contained within a foil-wrapped or brass cartridge case, with a maximum effective range of 200yd. One of the best performing and most accurate carbines of the Civil War era was the Maynard (**3**) which used an unprimed .50-caliber ball in a metallic cartridge. With an overall length of 36.5in, this weapon weighed only 6lb and had an effective range of 500yd. In service late in the war, the M1864 Remington carbine (**4**) had a "split-breech" action and used .50-caliber rim-fire cartridges. It was 34in in overall length, weighed 8.25lb, and had a maximum effective range of 500yd. Complete with patch box in the butt, the Type 1 M1858 Merrill carbine (**5**) was 37.25in in length and fired a .54-caliber ball with a niter-treated paper cartridge. It weighed 7.5lb and had an effective range of only 200yd. The Smith carbine (**6**) was a moderately successful weapon which fired a .50-caliber ball from a cartridge which could be made from paper, foil, or rubber. Weighing 7.5lb and 39.5in long, it broke like a shotgun to load. All of these weapons had a sling bar and ring on the left for attachment to a shoulder sling. (*Official Military Atlas of the Civil War*)

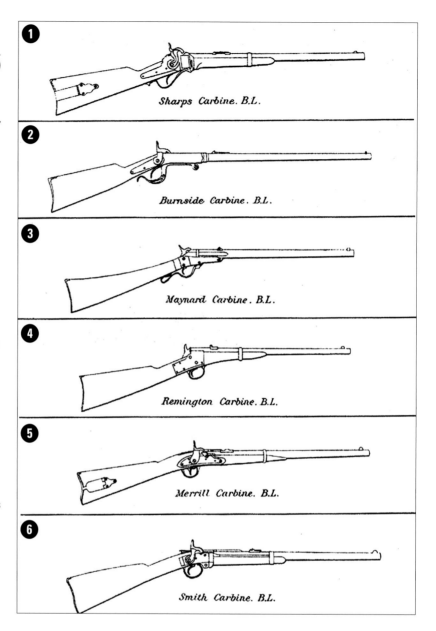

1 Sharps Carbine. B.L.

2 Burnside Carbine. B.L.

3 Maynard Carbine. B.L.

4 Remington Carbine. B.L.

5 Merrill Carbine. B.L.

6 Smith Carbine. B.L.

of laced bootees, although many troopers privately purchased knee-length boots. Sometimes the latter were issued to volunteer regiments. The main item of winter wear was a double-breasted overcoat which was usually sky blue in color, with standing collar and a cape that reached to the cuffs. At the beginning of the Civil War officers wore a dark-blue cloak coat closed at the front by four frogs and loops of black silk cord, but in November 1861 they were permitted to wear enlisted men's overcoats to make them less of a target in the field. Since 1857 a rubberized talma, or cloak, extending to the knee, with long sleeves, was issued for wet weather. About November 1861 this began to be replaced by a water-proofed poncho, despite the popularity of the talma.

Of the three main branches of service, some Union cavalry became the best armed. The carbine was a weapon peculiarly suited for use by mounted

troops. It proved superior to the shotgun and gave increased range and accuracy over the pistol. It could be used either mounted or dismounted and enabled dismounted cavalry to approximate the firepower of infantry. Single-shot carbines included the .52-caliber Sharps and .54-caliber Merrill which used paper or linen cartridges, while the .54-caliber Burnside had the advantage of firing fixed ammunition. Toward the end of the war several repeating carbines saw widespread service which gave the Union trooper a great advantage over his Confederate opponent. Among these, the .52-caliber Spencer was the most popular, using a magazine holding seven rim-fire cartridges in line in a spring-loaded metal tube inserted into the butt of the weapon. The Union Army purchased over 95,000 Spencer carbines by 1865.

The edged weapon carried by most Union cavalry was either the M1840 Heavy Cavalry (Dragoon) saber, nicknamed the "Old Wristbreaker," or the M1860 Light Cavalry version. Most cavalry were also armed with pistols, with the six-shot, .44-caliber Colt Army M1860 revolver seeing the most use. For example, of the 35 cavalry regiments in the Cavalry Corps of the Army of the Potomac on July 1, 1863, all but one was armed with this weapon. Other popular pistols included the .36-caliber Colt Old M1851 carried by regiments such as the 1st Rhode Island Cavalry, 2nd New Jersey Cavalry, and 1st, 5th, 6th, 10th, and 11th New York Cavalry. Also in use were the .36 and .44 Remington, and .44 LeFaucheux revolvers. Cartridge boxes of various sizes made of black bridle leather were issued to accommodate cavalry ammunition. That for the Pistol-Carbine had vertical loops on the rear and contained two tin inserts similar except for size to the 1855-pattern cartridge box for the rifle-musket. The Burnside carbine box had a wooden insert bored for 20 brass-cased cartridges, as did the Spencer box which had a capacity for 24 metallic cartridges.

Firing M1859 Sharps carbines, troopers of the 1st Maine Cavalry skirmish dismounted with Stuart's horsemen at the battle of Middleburg in June 1863. By this time only about three companies of the 1st Maine Cavalry were armed with carbines of which 112 men carried Sharps and 68 Burnside carbines. (Library of Congress LC-DIG-ppmsca-21121)

Confederate

As a result of General Orders No. 9 issued by the Adjutant and Inspector General's Office in Richmond, Virginia on June 6, 1861, cavalry of the

This plate depicts a trooper of the 1st Michigan Cavalry charging into the Confederate cavalry at Lewis Ford with his saber raised in the "For the head – Parry" position. This figure is based on 25-year-old Pvt Milo A. Thompson who was mustered in to Co. G, 1st Michigan Cavalry, on September 7, 1861, and survived unscathed a three-year term of service.

Weapons, dress, and equipment

Four hundred men in this man's regiment were armed with the single-shot 1st Model Lindner carbine (**1**) which fired a .56-caliber conical ball in a .58-caliber barrel. Weighing 6lb unloaded, this weapon had a maximum range of about 450yd, and an effective range of about 350yd. He is wielding a Model 1840 Heavy Cavalry saber (**2**), nicknamed the "Old Wristbreaker" because of its heavy flat-backed blade. This had a wire-wrapped leather-covered grip, and was 44in long with a 35in blade, and weighed approximately 2.5lb. It was designed for slashing when engaged at close quarters with the enemy. Accurate up to 75–100yd and weighing 2.65lb empty, his muzzle-loaded, cap and ball, single-action, .44-caliber Colt Army M1860 revolver rests in its 1860-pattern holster (**3**).

Typical of Union cavalrymen in 1862, the 1st Michigan Cavalry wore dark-blue full-dress wool jackets (**4**) trimmed with yellow; high-crowned 1859-pattern forage caps (**5**); sky-blue wool pants (**6**) with reinforced seat and inside leg; and Wellington-style calf boots (**7**). This trooper's accouterments consist of a black leather cavalry saber belt with 1851-pattern eagle plate (**8**), and hanger strap to help support the weight of the saber. Attached to this is an 1860-pattern "Universal" cartridge box (**9**) with belt loops and sling buckles and wood block drilled for .58-caliber carbine rounds; pistol-cartridge box

(**10**) carrying three packages of six revolver cartridges; and 1850-pattern percussion-cap pouch (not visible). The carbine is attached to a carbine sling (**11**) via a sling ring on the left side of the stock opposite the lock. An 1858-pattern canteen (**12**) with a capacity of 3 pints is slung over his right shoulder.

His 1859-pattern horse equipment consist of a McClellan saddle (**13**) with rolled overcoat secured via six leather straps in front of the pommel (**14**); rolled waterproof blanket (**15**) fastened via six leather straps to the cantle of the saddle; black leather stirrup straps (**16**), wooden stirrups and black leather stirrup hoods (**17**); canvas nose bag hanging from front off-side (**18**); black saddle bags (**19**) officially containing curry comb, brush, hoof-pick, cotton or linen huck rag, and horseshoes; tin mug (**20**) suspended from saddle bag on the off-side; separate bridle and halter (**21**); crupper strap (**22**); dark-blue dragoon horse blanket (**23**) with broad orange band around edge folded under the saddle; and wool web girth or surcingle (**24**) secured via leather strap with iron roller buckles, with same used as an improvised breast-strap (**25**). A carbine thimble (**26**) is attached to the surcingle "D" ring on the off-side of the saddle. Assuming the trooper weighs 150lb, this horse carries approximately 200lb into battle.

Confederacy's embryonic Regular Army were to wear a double-breasted tunic of cadet gray edged with yellow trim plus yellow facings on collar and cuffs, and sky-blue trousers. Headgear was clarified via General Orders No. 4 dated January 24, 1862, which described a French kepi with dark-blue band and yellow top. The tardiness in publication of these regulations, the expensive composition of the uniforms prescribed, and difficulties experienced by the general government in taking over any serious issue of clothing until late 1861, led to very few of these uniforms being produced and worn. However, the uniform regulations did accomplish several important things. They established a branch color system largely based on that used by the US Army, plus a pattern for buttons. They also set the style of dress of the Confederate officer. Most importantly, they did much to establish gray as the official color of the upper garment of the Confederate Army, in contrast with the dark blue being specified during the same period by most of their Northern counterparts.

Established by the Confederate government in February 1861, the commutation system stipulated that volunteers of the Provisional Army of the Confederate States were originally to provide their own clothing, for which they would receive $25 every six months. In many cases this money was transferred to state governments and volunteer aid societies who supplied the uniforms. Thus, the local womenfolk in hundreds of Southern towns and hamlets bought materials, and made coats, jackets, pants, and shirts for cavalrymen in the front line. Established by the Confederate Quartermaster Department by September 1861, the Clothing Bureau in Richmond began to provide uniforms throughout the next few years. Despite the fact that tunics were called for in the 1861 regulations, the gray jacket or "roundabout,"

much cheaper to produce, was issued. At first jackets received by cavalry were sometimes embellished with yellow cord but later war-issued examples were plain. When supplied, uniform caps were usually plain gray although hats of various colors were most commonly worn and were often of civilian origin. Issue trousers were gray, brown, or, in some instances, black. Uniforms were often unavailable to Confederate cavalry serving far from a supply line or Clothing Bureau, especially later in the war. Hence, troopers more often wore whatever clothing was available. This was mostly of civilian origin although items of captured Union uniform were also worn – especially overcoats and trousers.

Due to a massive shortage of arms, the Confederate cavalry volunteer was encouraged to supply his own weapon and most rode off to war carrying a multitude of weapons including shotguns, hunting rifles, flintlock muskets, and privately purchased martial arms such as Colt Army, Navy, and Pocket revolvers. Some fortunate troopers were later issued with carbines produced at the Richmond and Tallassee arsenals. According to Col (later Brig Gen) Thomas T. Munford, commanding the 2nd Virginia Cavalry:

When we entered the Confederate service we were armed with double barrel shotguns of every conceivable calibre, and our saddles and bridles were citizens' make of every conceivable shape, and wholly unsuited for cavalry service. When we laid down our arms we had as complete an outfit for each cavalryman in my brigade as we wanted, all of which had been supplied by the United States Quartermaster Department through their cavalry, and captured by us – the finest cavalry pistols, sabres, carbines, saddles, halters and bridles, blankets and canteens … in short, all that we wanted, and … all had the U.S. brand until [Brig Gen Thomas L.] Rosser's great disaster at Tom's Brook [on] 9th October, 1864. (Munford 1884–85: 348)

Pvt John P. Sellman, Co. K (2nd), 1st Virginia Cavalry, wears an example of a CS quartermaster-issue Richmond Depot, second-pattern jacket complete with shoulder straps. Running away from Brookville Academy in Maryland, Sellman enlisted in the Confederate Army at Fairfax Courthouse on September 1, 1861, and served with the 1st Virginia Cavalry until transferred to the 1st Maryland Cavalry on May 15, 1862. He has a holstered Colt revolver and cap pouch attached to his waist belt, and has Wellington-style calf-skin boots with straps either side to assist in pulling them on. (Courtesy of the USAMHI)

DRILL MANUALS AND TACTICS

Union

Based on the Napoleonic campaigns of the late 18th and early 19th centuries, the tactics and drill manuals used by the US Army during several decades prior to the Civil War were virtually unanimous in positing that the cavalry

This plate depicts a trooper of the 2nd Virginia Cavalry firing his shotgun during the cavalry battle at Lewis Ford. In firing to the front while mounted, cavalrymen were trained to aim directly over the horse's head as in that position a smaller target was offered to the enemy and the trooper's body was partly covered by the horse. The figure is based on a period photograph of Pvt Peter H. Bird of the Franklin Rangers (Co. D), 2nd Virginia Cavalry.

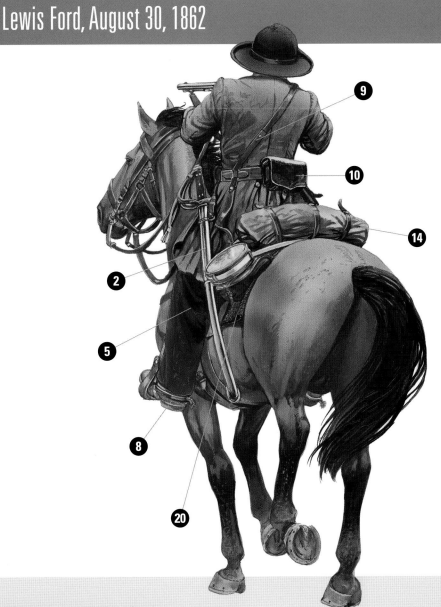

Weapons, dress and equipment

This trooper is firing a 20-gauge, double-barreled Baker shotgun (**1**), many of which were run through the blockade from England. Carried via a leather sling-strap attached to two swivel rings, it was shortened to carbine length, and weighed about 5lb. A close-quarter weapon, it had an effective range of only 7–17yd and fired "buck and ball" which consisted of buckshot combined with a single .69-caliber musket ball. His British 1853-pattern Light Cavalry saber (**2**) with buff-leather sword knot was also brought through the blockade, and weighed nearly 2.5lb with the scabbard and about 2lb without it. A muzzle-loading, cap and ball, single-action, .36-caliber Colt Navy M1851 revolver (**3**) weighing 2.63lb is carried in a holster attached to his sword belt.

He wears a gray frock coat (**4**) with yellow trim, dark-blue trousers (**5**), and black brimmed hat (**6**) with brass letters "FR" attached to the crown. All his buttons bear the Virginia state seal, as does his sword-belt plate (**7**). Footwear consists of brogans with sewn soles over which spurs are worn (**8**). His sword belt with hanger strap (**9**) supports a black-leather cartridge box (**10**), black-leather Colt Navy holster (**11**), and brown-leather cap pouch (**12**).

His horse equipment consists of a Richmond Arsenal Jenifer saddle (**13**) with rawhide-covered tree and leather skirts; a captured Federal overcoat (**14**) rolled and secured via six leather straps behind the cantle of the saddle; an arsenal-made three buckle bridle over a single ring halter, and a single rein loose ring curb bit (**15**); a brown-leather breast collar (**16**); a leather McClellan-style girth (**17**); and wooden stirrups minus hoods (**18**). His russet-leather saddle bags (**19**) are the "Crows Foot" or "Y" strap Richmond Arsenal pattern, and his saddle blanket (**20**) is made from woven Spanish moss which was a cheap alternative to wool. Assuming the trooper weighs 150lb, this horse is carrying roughly 190lb into combat.

Published in McClellan's *Regulations and Instructions for the Field Service of the United States Cavalry in Time of War* in 1861, this plate shows a cavalry regiment of five squadrons in "line of battle." The squadrons were formed from right to left in numerical order, with the colonel 25 paces (approximately 20yd) in front and center and chief bugler immediately behind him. The lieutenant colonel and major stood 12 paces (approximately 10yd) in front of the right and left wings of the regiment respectively. The company buglers formed in two ranks 25 paces to the rear of the regiment. The adjutant and sergeant major stood two paces to the right and left of the regiment respectively. The two general guides, with marker flags, were positioned at right and left rear of the regiment and in line with the file-closers. (Author's collection)

charge was crucial to success on the battlefield. Most of these works favored the double-rank formation also prescribed for an infantry attack, maintaining that the second rank increased the shock effect of the charge. They also held that two ranks would help close the gap when the first line made contact with the enemy and that the second rank would increase the number of sabers involved in the resulting melee. Such works also upheld the saber, rather than the pistol, as the proper attack weapon and emphasized the need to maintain close-order formation that also left space to permit the trooper to wheel to either side as conditions dictated.

The first major development in US cavalry training occurred in 1826 when a Board of Officers, with Maj Gen Winfield Scott as president and Lt Col Z. Taylor as a board member, was convened to produce *A system of tactics; or, Rules for the exercises and manoeuvres of the Cavalry and Light Infantry and Riflemen of the United States.* Published in 1834, this became known as *Scott's Tactics*, and included instruction on the training and equipment of the horse, plus the dismounted and mounted "School of the Trooper" and "School of the Squadron." Scott advocated a system where two companies, side by side, each in double rank, constituted a squadron with five squadrons in a regiment.

In 1839 2/Lt Philip Kearny and two other cavalry officers were sent by Secretary of War Joel R. Poinsett to Europe to study the organization and tactics of the French cavalry, thought to be the best in Europe. The three officers completed their mission after their return to the United States by writing the three-part *Cavalry Tactics*, also known as *Poinsett's Tactics*, which was an adaptation of a French dragoon manual. Published in four editions between 1841 and 1862, it also advocated the double-rank attack formation with a ten-company regiment organized into five squadrons. This served as the basis for later works, such as Henry Wager Halleck's *Elements of Military Art and Science*, first published in 1846, and remained the official cavalry manual throughout the Civil War period.

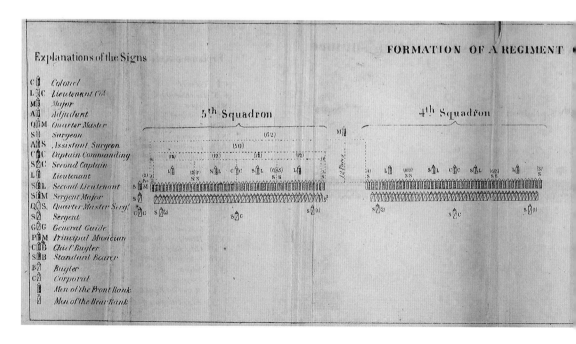

In 1855, while a captain in the 1st US Cavalry, George Brinton McClellan, along with Maj Richard Delafield and Maj Alfred Mordecai, was sent by Secretary of War Jefferson Davis on a mission to study "the practical working" of the changes which had been introduced into "the military systems ... of Europe" (Hillard 1865: 60). McClellan's report was finally published in 1861 as *Regulations and Instructions for the Field Service of the United States Cavalry in Time of War*. Also published in the same year was the two-volume *Cavalry Tactics, or, Regulations for the instruction, formations, and movements of the cavalry of the army and volunteers of the United States* by Philip St. George Cooke, then colonel of the 2nd US Dragoons. Cooke gave preference to a single-rank charge formation, prompted by his concern that double ranks were difficult to coordinate and prone to disorder. Although McClellan recommended the double-rank attack he gave conditional approval to Cooke's single-rank formation.

Although Cooke's system appeared to be advantageous, the War Department considered it too new and unproven to be taught to the Union cavalryman. Also, the wooded and mountainous Eastern Theater of the war did not always provide sufficient space for cavalry to operate in a single-rank formation. As a consequence, all but a few of the regiments in the Army of the Potomac adopted the double-rank formation. A notable exception was the Wolverine Brigade, composed of four Michigan regiments which served in the Army of the Potomac, mostly under Brig Gen George Armstrong Custer. For the first few months of their active service in 1863, the Wolverines launched themselves with some success at the enemy in the single-rank formation prescribed by Cooke. However, in early 1864 a War Office directive required them to adopt the two-rank system for which they successfully retrained, using the system during the remainder of the conflict.

Other works published on the eve of the Civil War included *Cavalry Drill and Sabre Exercise* by ex-Army officer George Patten, and *Authorized Cavalry Tactics, U.S.A.* by William Gilham, both of which were mere syntheses of earlier

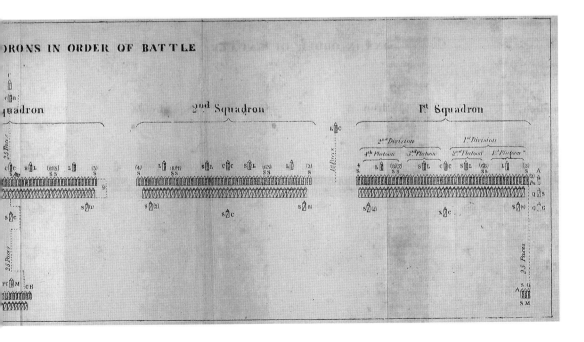

works. Also available was *Cavalry, its History and Tactics*, by British Army officer Capt L.E. Nolan of the 15th Hussars, and *Yeomanry Regulations ... Regulations for the Formation and Movements of the Cavalry*, by Lt-Col W.F. De Ros, published in London, England, in 1844. The manual most commonly used for the all-important training of cavalry horses was *Nolan's System for Training Cavalry Horses* by Capt Kenner Garrard, 5th US Cavalry, published in 1862.

Confederate

Although the Confederate War Department did not issue an official drill manual for its cavalry and used the same works as its Northern counterparts, several titles were in general use. These included *The Trooper's Manual: or, Tactics for light dragoons and mounted riflemen,* by J. Lucius Davis (1861), former Instructor in Cavalry Tactics at West Point and subsequently colonel of the 10th Virginia Cavalry; *Cavalry Drill and Sabre Exercise* (1862), which was a Southern reissue of Patten's 1861 work; and *A revised system of cavalry tactics, for the use of the cavalry and mounted infantry, C.S.A.* (1863), by Maj Gen Joseph Wheeler. The latter also advocated ten companies, each of which it termed a squadron, and, influenced by Cooke, employed the single-rank battle formation.

However, not all Confederate cavalry commanders agreed about the attack formation. Thomas Rosser preferred "the single rank formation to the double" as it was "more easily managed, and nothing like so many accidents occur," while Maj Gen Fitzhugh Lee recommended a compromise, stating, "My experience in the old United States army, as in the service of the Confederate States, is decidedly in favour of the double rank. You can never get ground sufficient to manoeuvre large bodies of cavalry by the single rank system ..." (quoted in Denison 1868: 103–04 & 352).

Most Confederate cavalrymen spent little time in a Camp of Instruction, and formal drill was not regularly conducted by many commanders. Recollecting his early war service, Capt Richard L.T. Beale, commanding Co. C, 9th Virginia Cavalry, stated, "No regular squad, company, or regimental drill had been generally adopted – and the supply of books of tactics was wholly inadequate to the wants of the officers" (Beale 1899: 15–16). The first training camps established in April 1861, such as Camp Lee at the Central Fairground near Richmond, Virginia, contained

Originally produced in 1855 and written by Samuel Cooper, Adjutant General of the US Army, this edition of *Cooper's Cavalry Tactics for the Use of Volunteers* was published in the South for the use of Confederate cavalry in 1861. As the front cover indicates, it also included "A Manual for Colt's Revolver" which aided officers and NCOs when conducting revolver drill. (Author's collection)

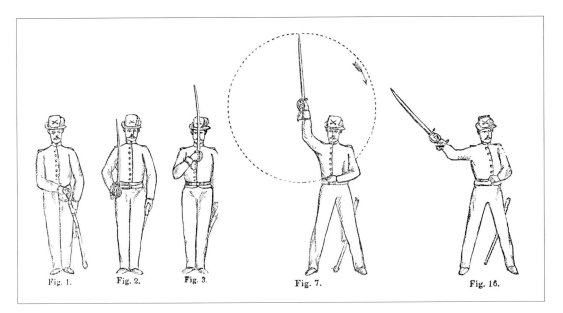

Fig. 1. Fig. 2. Fig. 3. Fig. 7. Fig. 16.

mixed commands of cavalry and infantry, and after a few days of basic training troops were quickly dispatched to the front. Cavalry training was taken somewhat more seriously in North Carolina where Camp Beauregard, at Ridgeway in Warren County, was designated as a regular school of cavalry instruction as early as July 1861. By and large the Southern cavalryman was dependent on an innate ability in horsemanship.

Cavalry troopers were formed into "sets of four" for drill and combat purposes. All of the actions shown in these engravings from George Patten's *Cavalry Drill and Sabre Exercise*, published in 1862, were practically the same when mounted. "The Sabre Exercise" Figs 1 and 2 illustrate "Draw – Sabre," Fig. 3 shows "Present – Sabre," Fig. 7 demonstrates "Rear – Moulinet," and Fig. 16 the beginning of the movement "Left – Cut." (Author's collection)

CONDUCT IN BATTLE

The basic formation for both Union and Confederate cavalry was "column by fours" which was narrow and flexible, and could usually pass most obstacles and deploy easily to the left or right. Occasionally a column of twos was employed, and even single file in woodland, especially if a small unit wished to appear larger to the enemy at a distance. When deploying into line of battle the regiment followed the command "left into line" or "right into line," dependent on which direction it was required to form. Most verbal orders were transmitted from officers to the chief bugler who sounded the command which was then echoed by the company buglers. Bugle calls on the battlefield included "Forward," "Trot," "Gallop," "Charge," "To the Left," "To the Right," "Come About," "Halt," "Disperse," "Commence Firing," "Cease Firing," and "Rally on the Officer."

The rates of movement of a cavalry regiment on campaign and in battle were 4mph at the walk; 6mph at a slow trot; 8mph when maneuvering at a trot; 12mph at a maneuvering gallop; and 16mph at full extended gallop. Cavalry on the march would occupy a considerable space. A company in column of fours could stretch back 95yd and a regiment might take up nearly ¾ mile of road. Although up to 35 miles per day could be covered with ease, this could be pushed to far greater distances and troopers did sleep in the saddle on forced marches. During Stuart's raid on Chambersburg in 1862, his command marched 80 miles in 27 hours, while in 1864 the Union divisions of Wilson and Kautz marched 300 miles in ten days.

Entitled "Music on Sheridan's line of battle," this wood engraving is based on a post-war sketch by Isaac Walton Taber. At the beginning of the war both Union and Confederate cavalry regiments were often accompanied by a brass band. While considered essential for dress parade, guard mount, reviews, and other special occasions, bands were generally regarded at Union Army headquarters as an expensive luxury and were soon disbanded. However, continued requests for cavalry music sometimes resulted in a compromise and musicians were selected from the enlisted men of the regiment without expense to the government. According to Bugler H.P. Moyer, 17th Pennsylvania Cavalry, "The inspiring music of 'Yankee Doodle,' 'Hail Columbia,' 'Marching Through Georgia,' 'John Brown's Body,' 'All Quiet along the Potomac,' 'Tenting on the Old Camp Ground,' and songs of that kind, put the fighting spirit into the boys in blue, just the same as 'Dixie,' and 'My Maryland,' inspirited the boys who wore the gray" (Moyer 1911: 303). (*Battles & Leaders*)

The charge was considered the decisive action of cavalry but required thorough training of both men and horses. *Poinsett's Tactics* stated that, in order to be successful, it must "be short, the horses should be urged to the quickest gallop, without losing command of them, and the men should remain united and masters of their movements, not withstanding the quickness of the pace." This did not always happen. For example, at Trevilian Station on June 11, 1864, elements of Custer's Michigan brigade charged several miles beyond its original starting point after crashing through dismounted Confederate cavalry and galloped far beyond the center of action before the horses could be reined in and the unit re-formed. Led by Lt Col Russell A. Alger, the surviving troopers completed a circuitous route of a farther 20 miles before finding safety inside friendly lines (Wittenberg 2001: 109).

As dictated by the drill books, the charge was usually conducted in two ranks but could also be done in column by four, double columns by four, or even triple columns by four. As the war progressed cavalry commanders learned to reconnoiter the ground to make sure it was suitable for a charge, as rough terrain or fences and hedges would break ranks and cause the unit to lose momentum or halt altogether. Although Stuart had ample opportunity to do this before the charge at Buckland Mills on October 19, 1863, the columns on both his flanks were badly obstructed by fences and ditches, putting two-thirds of his command out of much of the action.

Cavalry charges against infantry became less successful during the course of the war due to advances in technology which introduced more accurate and deadlier weapons such as the rifle-musket. However, the development and mass production of breech-loading carbines by 1864 enabled the Union cavalryman, and to a lesser extent his Confederate counterpart, to fight dismounted against both infantry and cavalry when required. In this formation cavalry could take and hold ground until infantry support arrived, cover gaps in a battle line, or serve as a rearguard during a retreat. In order to deploy a dismounted cavalry regiment in combat, every fourth man was designated a horse holder and retired to the rear with four mounts in his care.

These men took advantage of any natural obstacles such as trees, rocks, and hollows in the ground, but were always readily available for the dismounted troopers to mount up quickly. Meanwhile, skirmishers were pushed out in open order in front of the main body of dismounted troopers as the regiment engaged with the enemy.

The main role of the cavalry in both armies was that of scouting and protecting the flanks of the main force. The purpose of outpost duty was twofold – to establish a flexible screen against infiltration from the enemy, and to watch and report enemy movements. Cavalry on "Grand Guard" or outlying picket duty were posted in front and on both flanks of an army at a distance of about 500yd. One third of a Grand Guard remained ready to mount at a moment's notice, while the rest unbridled their horses. Single vedettes, or sentries, were placed a farther 500yd beyond this at points from where they could see an approaching enemy and observe one another. Patrols moved continuously from Grand Guard to vedettes and might probe several miles beyond the latter. When coming in contact with the enemy, the Grand Guard had to retire as slowly as possible and skirmish constantly in order to give the main body of troops time to turn out and prepare for combat.

Cavalry served as the eyes of both Union and Confederate armies from the beginning of the war. On June 5, 1861, an infantryman in the 13th New York wrote from camp at Arlington Heights, Virginia, "There is a cavalry company here, called the Texan Rangers, who go out on scouting expeditions every night, reconnoitering the enemy's camp." Based on an original sketch probably produced by Eyre Crowe, this engraving was published in the *Illustrated London News* on September 14 of the same year with the caption "Texan Rangers (Federalists) reconnoitering between Alexandria and Fairfax, Virginia." This company possibly consisted of volunteers who came east from Texas and California to fight for the Union. (Author's collection)

Lewis Ford

August 30, 1862

BACKGROUND TO BATTLE

Following the collapse of Maj Gen George B. McClellan's Peninsula Campaign after the Seven Days' Battles of June 1862, Maj Gen John Pope was appointed to command the newly organized Army of Virginia, which was assembled from scattered Union forces in the Shenandoah Valley and Northern Virginia. Meanwhile, McClellan's Army of the Potomac was ordered to evacuate the Peninsula and join Pope, who also commanded the troops under Maj Gen Franz Sigel (I Corps, Army of Virginia), Maj Gen Nathaniel Banks (II Corps, Army of Virginia), and Maj Gen Irvin McDowell (III Corps, Army of Virginia). With this combined force, Pope was charged with the threefold mission of protecting Washington, DC, defending the Shenandoah Valley, and drawing Confederate forces away from McClellan's evacuation operation by advancing in the direction of Gordonsville and Charlottesville. The 5,000 cavalrymen in his Army of Virginia were organized into three brigades under Brig Gen John P. Hatch, Brig Gen George D. Bayard, and Col John Beardsley, and were described by Pope himself as "badly mounted and armed and in poor condition for service" (*OR* I, XII, 2: 20).

Taking advantage of the situation, Lee decided to strike first while Pope and McClellan had still not joined forces. Reorganizing his army of about 55,000 men into two "wings" or commands, with the left wing under Maj Gen Thomas "Stonewall" Jackson, and the right commanded by Maj Gen

James Longstreet, he saw an opportunity to destroy Pope before McClellan could join him. Sending Jackson's 14,000 troops, plus the Cavalry Division under Maj Gen J.E.B. Stuart, toward Gordonsville to block the Federal advance and protect the Virginia Central Railroad, he also committed Maj Gen A.P. Hill to join Jackson with 12,000 men. Longstreet's right wing remained to protect the Confederate capital.

In early August 1862, Pope marched south into Culpeper County, Virginia, toward Gordonsville. On the 9th of that month, Banks' corps clashed with Jackson's larger force at Cedar Mountain in Culpeper County. Although the Federals gained an early advantage, a Confederate counterattack led by Hill repulsed Banks' troops. Still awaiting the arrival of McClellan's troops from the Peninsula, Pope took up a position at the convergence of the Rapidan and Rappahannock rivers in a V-shaped area northwest of Fredericksburg and approximately 50 miles north of Richmond. This location provided a natural defense against an enemy approaching from the south, but represented a potential trap for defenders if attacked from the west. Sensing the opportunity for a swift victory, Lee began to maneuver his army into position to pounce upon the unsuspecting Army of Virginia.

Meanwhile, on August 16, a detachment – composed of elements of the 5th New York Cavalry and 1st Michigan Cavalry under Col Thornton F. Brodhead, executive officer of the latter regiment – of Brig Gen John Buford's cavalry brigade went on a raid toward Verdiersville, the location of Stuart's headquarters. Although Stuart managed to escape, the Union troopers found a letter from Lee to Stuart disclosing his plans to attack Pope's exposed left flank at the confluence of the two rivers. Thus Pope was alerted to the peril he faced and withdrew back east across the Rappahannock River. In a retaliatory raid at Catlett's Station on August 22, Confederate cavalry intercepted orders that provided Lee with valuable intelligence concerning reinforcements arriving from the Peninsula for Pope's army. Realizing he had lost a valuable opportunity and now faced a much larger Union force of 70,000 men with his army of only 55,000, Lee's new plan was to send Jackson and Stuart on a 50-mile flanking march to strike at Pope's rear, with Stuart's cavalry and the brigade of Brig Gen Beverly H. Robertson, consisting of the 2nd, 6th, 7th, and 12th Virginia Cavalry, leading the way.

After passing around Pope's right flank via Thoroughfare Gap on August 26, Jackson reached the railroad at Bristoe Station and before daybreak the next day moved on to capture and destroy the massive Union supply depot at Manassas Junction. After a day of wild feasting, Jackson's men burned what remained of the Federal supplies and moved to a defensive position in the

Serving as a second lieutenant in the 2nd US Dragoons before the Civil War, John Buford, Jr. was influenced by the military philosophy of Brig Gen John Watts de Peyster, who believed that the skirmish line should become the new line of battle. Appointed Assistant Inspector General in the Union Army with the rank of major in November 1861, he served within the Washington defenses until promoted to brigadier general in July 1862 when he was given command of the Cavalry Brigade, II Corps, Army of Virginia, by Maj Gen John Pope. He personally led the charge of the 1st Michigan Cavalry at Lewis Ford on August 30, 1862, and was wounded in the knee by a spent bullet. He went on to serve with distinction as a divisional commander and is credited with selecting the field of battle at Gettysburg on June 30, 1863. He died of typhoid fever in December 1863. (US National Archives – 111-B-2710)

This youthful Virginia cavalryman has crossed-sabers brass insignia over a company letter "A" attached to his hat. His jacket is trimmed around collar and cuffs, and unusually has an 11-button front. A Colt revolver is tucked into a captured Union waist belt fastened by a New York plate with the letters "N Y" in old-script letters. Confederate commanders positively encouraged their men to capture what arms and equipage they could in order to make up for the increasingly limited supply of Confederate-manufactured material. (Courtesy of Dan Schwab)

woods at Groveton near the old 1861 Manassas battlefield. In response, an infuriated Pope abandoned his line along the Rappahannock and headed toward Manassas to crush Jackson. At the same time, Lee marched north with Longstreet's corps to reunite his army. In order to prevent Union forces from concentrating at Centreville, and to bring Pope to battle, Jackson ordered his troops to attack the Union column as it marched north along the Warrenton Turnpike toward Groveton during the late afternoon of August 28. This savage firefight near Brawner's Farm lasted for several hours until nightfall and resulted in a stalemate.

Convinced that Jackson was isolated, and sure that he could destroy him before Lee and Longstreet intervened, Pope ordered his columns to converge on Groveton. On August 29, Pope's army found Jackson's men deployed in an unfinished railroad cut north of the Warrenton Turnpike. In a series of uncoordinated attacks which lasted throughout the afternoon, Pope hurled his men against the Confederates. In several places his troops momentarily breached Jackson's line, but each time they were thrown back.

Earlier that day, Buford's cavalry had been posted with Brig Gen James Ricketts' Second Division of McDowell's corps at Warrenton, to protect the rear of the army. At about 0930hrs, Buford's scouts spotted the approach of a huge Confederate column and a dispatch was sent to Ricketts stating, "A large force from Thoroughfare Gap is making a junction through Gainesville up the Centreville road with the forces in the direction of the cannonading" (*OR* I, XII, 3: 730). At 1130hrs, Ricketts forwarded the dispatch to Col Edmund Schriver, McDowell's chief of staff, who dutifully informed his corps commander. For reasons that remain unclear to this day, McDowell failed to forward the dispatch to Pope until 1900hrs that day. After the war, McDowell would demand a court of inquiry to clear his name as a result of his poor performance at Second Manassas and his failure to inform Pope of the approach of Longstreet which ultimately led to the Union defeat the next day.

Longstreet's troops began to arrive on the battlefield during the afternoon of August 29 and, unknown to Pope, were deployed on Jackson's right and overlapping the exposed Union left flank. Lee urged Longstreet to attack several times, but "Old Pete" refused, maintaining that the time was not yet right. As the fighting continued, Ricketts' division and Buford's cavalry marched toward the sound of the guns to rejoin the main army, and passed through Manassas Junction around midday proceeding on to the battlefield

This cavalry orderly was photographed near Antietam, Maryland, by Alexander Gardner in October 1862. He wears a four-button sack coat, hat of probable civilian origin, and tall boots with knee flaps, and carries an M1860 Light Cavalry saber in metal scabbard. The complete set of horse equipments for a Union cavalryman was listed in the US 1861 *Ordnance Manual* as consisting of "1 bridle, 1 watering bridle, 1 halter, 1 saddle, 1 pair of saddle bags, 1 saddle blanket, 1 surcingle, 1 pair of spurs, 1 curry comb, 1 horse brush, 1 picket pin, and 1 lariat (1 link and 1 nose-bag, when specially required)." (Library of Congress LC-DIG-cwpb-01143)

about 1530hrs, where they spent the next few hours on picket duty in the area of Pope's headquarters on Buck Hill north of the Stone House.

During the night of August 29, Jackson drew his lines closer to those of Longstreet, thereby abandoning some of his trenches. The next morning passed quietly. Observing the empty positions at his front, Pope mistakenly believed that the Confederates were retreating and ordered his army forward, only to discover that Lee stood firm. Undeterred and still unaware of the presence of Longstreet's corps, he ordered yet another attack against Jackson's line which again held, and the Federals were thrown back in a bloody repulse. At about 1400hrs Maj Gen John F. Reynolds, commanding the Pennsylvania Reserve Division (III Corps, Army of Virginia), finally observed Longstreet's presence and realized the danger Pope's army was in. Running the gauntlet of Confederate shell and sniper fire, he personally reported this to Pope. Unconvinced that his army was in such imminent peril, the Union commander ordered Buford to conduct a cavalry scout to see if the enemy was indeed about to turn his left flank. Taking the 1st Michigan Cavalry, 1st Vermont Cavalry, and 1st West Virginia Cavalry, Buford spent some time vainly searching for signs of Longstreet. Sgt Stephen A. Clark, Co. F, 1st Vermont Cavalry, recalled, "We discovered nothing and were returning, when nearing a piece of woods, like a thunder clap, came volley after volley of musketry and then a charge of the enemy on our infantry. Our lines gave way, and soon were in full retreat" (*NT* Jun 21, 1888, 3:3). As Longstreet attacked, Buford led his cavalry back toward the rear of the Union army and eventually halted near "Portici," the farm house owned by Francis Lewis, which stood on a ridge overlooking Bull Run and had served as Beauregard's headquarters on July 21, 1861. His troopers were there only a short time before they became involved in a critical stage in the Union retreat.

MAP KEY

1 1700hrs (approx.): Following the attack of Longstreet's corps on the Federal left flank, Robertson's cavalry brigade is ordered to ride around the extreme right of the Confederate position to block one of the anticipated Union routes of retreat at Lewis Ford across Bull Run.

2 1715hrs (approx.): Leading the Confederate column Col Munford, commanding the 2nd Virginia Cavalry, spies the 4th New York Cavalry resting their horses and, believing it was only "a squadron or two" of the enemy, orders two companies under Lt Col Watts to charge them.

3 1720hrs (approx.): The men of the 4th New York Cavalry mount up and fall back to join Buford's brigade drawn up in "line of battle" along a ridge on the Lewis Farm. Watts' two companies halt in the face of greater numbers.

4 1722hrs (approx.): Buford orders the 1st Michigan Cavalry to charge while Munford is forming the rest of his regiment in line of battle to support Watts, catching the 2nd Virginia Cavalry off guard.

5 1725hrs (approx.): Munford orders the 2nd Virginia Cavalry to charge into the oncoming 1st Michigan Cavalry, and the two regiments clash head-on.

6 1730hrs (approx.): A courier is sent to Robertson who orders forward the rest of his brigade with the 12th Virginia Cavalry at the head of the column followed by the 7th Virginia Cavalry, with the 6th Virginia Cavalry in reserve.

7 1735hrs (approx.): Robertson's brigade charges into the 1st Michigan Cavalry standing in "line of battle" to the right of the Lewis farmhouse. The Michiganders break and run.

8 1736hrs (approx.): The 7th Virginia Cavalry veers to the right and charges at the flank of the 4th New York Cavalry, which also breaks and runs.

9 1740hrs (approx.): Most of the scattered Union troopers escape through the woods skirting Bull Run, cross at Lewis Ford, and gallop north to join the main Union column retreating along the Warrenton Turnpike. Col Brodhead is killed.

10 1745hrs (approx.): Robertson's troopers pursue Buford's routed brigade toward the Warrenton Turnpike but withdraw when they encounter the 1st Vermont Cavalry and artillery fire.

Battlefield environment

The cavalry battlefield at Second Manassas consisted of gentle rolling hills which formed broad, low ridges and extensive "flat" uplands dissected by deep gulleys and shallow, sluggish streams, the largest of which was Holkum Branch, a tributary of Bull Run. The contested area lay within the southeast quadrant formed by the crossroads of the Warrenton Turnpike and Sudley Road with Bull Run to the east. The land around the Henry and Robinson farms in the north was composed of old pastures and once-cultivated fields broken by patchy pine and virgin oak woodland. The terrain south of this consisted of thicker woodland while rolling pasture surrounded the Lewis Farm and made up the approaches to the Lewis Ford. Several unnamed roads dissected the area from north to south, and the old Warrenton Road formed a southern boundary. Most of this area was heavily scarred by the battle fought there on July 21, 1861.

Records indicate that the weather was hot and steamy, with temperatures around 90 degrees Fahrenheit each day toward the end of August 1862. This caused dust clouds with each movement of massed cavalry during the events which transpired during the next few days. As happened after First Manassas/Bull Run, the battle on August 30, 1862, culminated in rain which according to the *Richmond Examiner* "fell quite heavily" (*RE* Sep 1, 1862: 1:4).

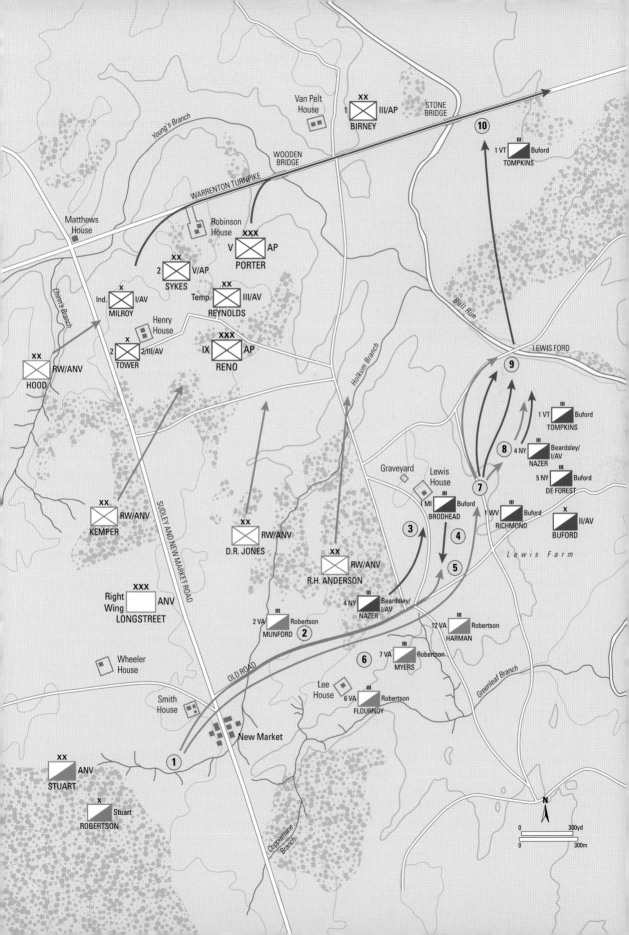

Van Pelt
House

STONE
BRIDGE

1 ⊠ III/AP
BIRNEY

(10)

1 VT ⊟ Buford
TOMPKINS

Young's Branch

WOODEN
BRIDGE

WARRENTON TURNPIKE

Matthews
House

Robinson
House

XXX
⊠ AP
PORTER

Bull Run

Chinn's Branch

2 ⊠ V/AP
SYKES

Ind. x
⊠ I/AV
MILROY

Temp. ⊠ III/AV
REYNOLDS

LEWIS FORD

Henry
House

(9)

x
2 ⊠ 2/III/AV
TOWER

XXX
IX ⊠ AP
RENO

Holkum Branch

1 VT ⊟ Buford
TOMPKINS

XX
⊠ RW/ANV
HOOD

(8) 4 NY ⊟ Beardsley/
NAZER I/AV

5 NY ⊟ Buford
DE FOREST

Graveyard

Lewis
House

(7)

XX
⊠ RW/ANV
KEMPER

1 MI ⊟ Buford
BRODHEAD

1 WV ⊟ Buford
RICHMOND

x
⊟ II/AV
BUFORD

XX
⊠ RW/ANV
D.R. JONES

(3)

(4)

Lewis Farm

SUDLEY AND NEW MARKET ROAD

XX
⊠ RW/ANV
R.H. ANDERSON

(5)

XXX
☐ ANV
Right
Wing
LONGSTREET

4 NY ⊟ Beardsley/
NAZER I/AV

2 VA ⊟ Robertson
MUNFORD (2)

12 VA ⊟ Robertson
HARMAN

Wheeler
House

OLD ROAD

7 VA ⊟ Robertson
MYERS

(6)

Greenleaf Branch

Lee
House

Smith
House

6 VA ⊟ Robertson
FLOURNOY

New Market

(1)

XX
⊟ ANV
STUART

x
⊟ Stuart
ROBERTSON

Coppermine Branch

N

0   300yd
0   300m

INTO COMBAT

As he observed the ensuing chaos in the Union ranks from his headquarters on Henry Hill, Lee sensed the opportunity for a decisive victory and ordered Stuart's cavalry forward. As a result, Stuart instructed Robertson's brigade, which stood west of New Market and to the left of the Sudley Road, to ride around the extreme right of the Confederate position to perform the classic role of cavalry by blocking one of the anticipated Union routes of retreat, which was a crossing point on Bull Run called Lewis Ford. Of the experience of these mounted troops up to that point, Pvt Fay, 7th Virginia Cavalry, later recollected:

All day long we lay in the rear of our "incomparable infantry," resting on the hills overlooking the low grounds and interminable woods in which the battle raged. The booming of cannon on all sides became monotonous, but toward evening it was varied by the rattle of musketry, which extended in louder and louder peals along the lengthening line. We could hear the yells and cheers of the combatants as they charged back and forth over the fields below or, unseen by us, in the woods beyond. The atmosphere became charged with smoke, and the very air grew oppressive. (Fay 1915: 264)

25-year-old Pvt Peter H. Bird of the Franklin Rangers (Co. D), 2nd Virginia Cavalry, had recently returned to the ranks having recovered from typhoid fever. He was killed in action at Crampton's Gap in Maryland just 17 days after taking part in the fighting at the Lewis Farm. (Library of Congress LC-DIG-ppmsca-34335)

Owing to hard service, lack of rations, assignment to special duties, and horse detail, Robertson's brigade was greatly diminished in numbers, having only about 400 troopers present that day. Pvt Fay stated:

To give one an idea how attenuated my regiment had become in consequence of severe marching and the lack of subsistence, it is only necessary to state that only eighty men constituted the rank and file of the 7th Virginia when it formed in line for duty on that eventful afternoon. My company (F) mustered but eight men in ranks, under its only officer present, [2nd] Lieutenant (afterwards Captain) [Isaac] Kuykendall. This would have been very humiliating to us but for the fact that our company had double the number of men that the company in our front could muster on that occasion. One lieutenant and four men were all that Company E carried into the fight ... (Fay 1915: 264)

Robertson's troopers received the order to mount up at about 1700hrs. Commanded by Col Thomas T. Munford, the 2nd Virginia Cavalry advanced first, cantering along the Old Road in the direction of the Lewis Farm with Robertson at its head. Munford's troopers saw no sign of the enemy until they reached the ridge overlooking Bull Run. However, ahead of them the 4th New York Cavalry (First Regiment, German Cavalry), of Beardsley's brigade, was operating as part of the Union rearguard attempting to rally stragglers. At about 1715hrs this regiment had halted in a stand of woods to rest their horses when Munford's approach was observed and hastily reported to the commanding officer, Lt Col Ferries Nazer. At the head of his column, Robertson saw "a company of the enemy's cavalry" at his front, and ordered Lt Col James W. Watts,

2nd Virginia Cavalry, to charge with the Campbell Rangers (Co. I) and Clay Troop (Co. A), which could not have amounted to more than 30 to 40 men (Driver & Howard 1995: 56–57). Mounting up hastily, the men of the 4th New York Cavalry withdrew about a half-mile until they reached Buford's brigade of about 1,500 troopers which was drawn up on a ridge in the fields of the Lewis Farm, with some men in the saddle and others dismounted. The 1st Michigan Cavalry stood mounted in a single line about 200yd in front of the main body of Union cavalry which was concealed in a line of trees beyond the brow of the hill about a half-mile in advance of the Lewis Ford. In his after-battle report Nazer stated, "I informed General Buford of the enemy's whereabouts and intentions, and at his request quickly reformed my command into line behind the 1st Michigan Cavalry ..." (*OR* I, XII, 2: 274).

According to Col Munford, Watts' two companies halted at the sight of the larger Union force. Close enough to hear the command to the Union troopers, "Forward, trot," but still believing that he faced only a squadron or two of enemy cavalry, Munford prepared the rest of his command to launch a saber charge to go to the aid of his second-in-command (Driver 1991: 57). His report continued, "As soon as I had formed my line of battle I determined to move to the rear for a better position; but as soon as I commenced this move the enemy, mistaking my object, advanced upon me." Reacting quickly, Munford wheeled as many of his men as possible to "the right-about by fours and went at them with drawn sabers" (*OR* I, XII, 2: 748).

Meanwhile, Buford steadied his men by calling out, "Boys, save our army, cover their retreat!" and his troopers responded with three hearty cheers (*DFP* Sep 13, 1862: 2:1). Riding out to the front, he next issued the command for

In this photograph by George Barnard a group of children stare at a patrol of seven Union cavalry troopers lined up at Sudley Ford across Bull Run in Virginia. The devastation caused by battle is much in evidence in their gaunt surroundings and illustrates the type of terrain in which the cavalry fight at Lewis Ford took place on August 30, 1862. (Library of Congress LC-DIG-cwpb-00955)

the 1st Michigan Cavalry to trot forward into "line of battle by fours, front into line." One trooper recalled, "The men came up in fine style … I held my breath for a moment, for this was our first charge. I thought of home and friends. The bugle sounded the charge, and away we went …" (quoted in Robertson 1882: 565). Observing the charge from about 150yd away as a prisoner of war, hospital steward D.O. Pickard, 2nd US Sharpshooters, related, "The boys rode splendidly, knee to knee, in perfect line … At the command, 'Draw sabers!' every blade flashed at the same instant" (*NT* Oct 15, 1885: 4:5). A correspondent of the *New-York Tribune* who also witnessed the scene wrote, "… the bugle sounded, and over the hill galloped our men to meet the advancing Rebels. As our men approached them, the Rebel cavalry discharged double-barreled shot-guns, and then met us in full charge" (*NYT* Sep 2, 1862: 8:3). Pickard added:

> The rebs drew their revolvers, the Federal line started an instant first, and they rushed right together, each line passing through the other, except those who went down in the shock of collision. Then each man of each side attempted to get back to their original position, and the shooting and running, cursing and cutting that followed cannot be understood except by an eye witness. (*NT* Oct 15, 1885: 4:5)

Milo A. Thompson was a 25-year-old house-painter resided in Pontiac, Michigan, when he enlisted in Co. G, 1st Michigan Cavalry, on September 7, 1861. Fighting at Lewis Ford and most of the other engagements his regiment was involved in, he re-enlisted at Stevensburg, Virginia, on December 21, 1863, and was finally discharged from the Army on July 30, 1865. (Courtesy of Kristy Wilson)

Of the attempted Confederate countercharge Munford stated, "My regiment in line of battle going at a gallop, we went through the first line of the enemy and engaged part of the second. Here a terrible hand-to-hand fight ensued. The two commands were thoroughly intermingled, and the enemy overpowering us by numbers (being at least four to one), we were driven back" (*OR* I, XII, 2: 748). A Confederate casualty of the initial clash, Pvt Thornton R. Baxter of the Albemarle Light Horse (Co. K), 2nd Virginia Cavalry, wrote later, "Our regiment charged four regiments of yankee cavalry and they charging at the same time. We had a regular hand to hand sabre fight …" Baxter's horse was killed in the melee, and his leg injured when the animal fell on him (Driver 1991: 57). Munford's mount was also slain and, according to Col Asher W. Harman, 12th Virginia Cavalry, he was "severely thrashed over the back with a sabre …" (Hotchkiss Papers). Munford merely reported, "I was dismounted by a lick, but not seriously hurt" (*OR* I, XII, 2: 748). Elsewhere, Lt Col Watts received eight saber cuts; Maj Cary Breckenridge sustained four saber cuts, one in the face; 2/Lt Robert H. Kelso (Co. A) suffered five saber cuts; and 2/Lt William W. Walton (Co. C) three. Total casualties in the regiment amounted to three killed and 45 wounded. Munford later stated, "Had my regiment been promptly reinforced my command would not have suffered so severely" (*OR* I, XII, 2: 748).

Thus, the charge by the 2nd Virginia was broken and sent reeling back. Although this was one of the

first occasions when Union cavalry dared to charge their Southern counterparts, its success was unfortunately short-lived as Buford failed to consolidate his success. Although he re-formed the 1st Michigan Cavalry and 4th New York Cavalry atop the ridge, he left his two remaining regiments, the 1st West Virginia Cavalry and 1st Vermont Cavalry, undeployed behind the crest of the hill, choosing to meet the inevitable renewed Confederate attack with only half his command.

Receiving word via a courier from Robertson that he had encountered the enemy in force and was in urgent need of support, Stuart quickly ordered forward the 12th and 7th Virginia Cavalry, with the 6th Virginia Cavalry behind them in reserve. Standing near Henry House Hill, the 12th Virginia Cavalry received its order to advance just as the wounded of the 2nd Virginia Cavalry began to pass by. Col Harman wrote later, "From the sabre cuts I saw on the faces and over the heads of his men, it was a gallant charge and had been bravely met" (Hotchkiss Papers). Of his advance toward the action, Pvt Fay of the 7th Virginia Cavalry wrote:

> The sounds of a conflict we could not see fell upon our ears, and as the 12th Virginia moved rapidly up the hill we prepared to follow it. Just then Colonel [Thomas S.] Flournoy, of the 6th, sought to lead his regiment in ahead of the 7th, but was halted by [Capt Samuel B.] Myers, who, shaking his head, said: "No, no; the 7th is next in line and will be next in the charge." There was little interval, either of time or space, between the regiments in the forward movement. When the 7th reached the crest of the hill we could see where the intrepid Munford, of the 2d Virginia, had met and broken the enemy's ranks after his leading squadron had been badly shattered in the first onslaught. There was an old abandoned field to the right

The chaos of the Union retreat across the Stone Bridge at Second Bull Run/Manassas is captured in this lithograph by *Harper's Weekly* illustrator Rufus F. Zogbaum, published in 1885. With a total of 13,830 Union combatants killed, wounded, and missing, the battle was seen as a stunning Confederate victory which convinced many that the Southern armies, including their cavalry, were superior to those of the North. Having been worsted at Lewis Ford, a detachment of Buford's troopers can be seen joining the column in the background. (*Battles & Leaders*)

of where the road went over the hill, and there the combat had taken place. The dead and wounded of both sides lay scattered about, riderless horses were dashing here and there, and the deep gulleys which frequent rains had cut into the hillside were filled at places with men and horses, struggling to extricate themselves. It had evidently been a fierce and bloody hand-to-hand encounter, though of brief duration. (Fay 1915: 264)

Of the moment the 12th Virginia Cavalry dashed into battle, its commander Asher Harman later wrote: "I did not have time to even form my regiment in platoons, for Col. Broadhead [sic] with the 1st Michigan Cavalry was in perfect order on the brow of the hill ... to the right of the Lewis House" (OR I, XII, 2: 752). Harman ordered his men to form into line of battle on the first set of fours and to charge. Riding behind them in command of the understrength 7th Virginia Cavalry as the senior company-grade officer, Pennsylvania-born Samuel Myers recalled:

When [the] head of our regiment came to [the] top of [the] hill on our right the enemy were drawn up in line of battle on an opposite hill about 400 yards distant, their line extending a considerable distance on [the] left, when the Second and Twelfth engaged [the] enemy. I ordered [the] regiment to charge with drawn sabers on their right flank, which the whole command obeyed with the greatest alacrity, charging upon them with shouts that made the very Weldon ring ... (OR I, XII, 2: 752)

According to Pvt Fay, of Co. F, "The men of our brigade, now intermingled and in wedgelike form, dashed headlong toward the battle line of blue; and as the apex of this swiftly moving mass was about to pierce the center of their line, it wavered for an instant, then broke and fled in every direction" (Fay 1915: 265).

The initial numerical superiority enjoyed by Buford's troopers evaporated once Robertson threw his entire brigade into the fray. Harman wrote, "My regiment responded to the order [to charge] with such spirit and vim that I pierced Broadhead's [sic] center, shivered his regiment, and drove him back on his supports in such confusion that I had them all on the run ..." (OR I, XII, 2: 752). One Michigander stated, "From that time on there was no order or organization ... but one mixed mass of ... men dismounted and horses without riders ... all trying to get away" (quoted in Hennessy 1999: 433–34). 1/Sgt William P. Wilkin, Co. F, 1st West Virginia Cavalry, recalled, "I was in the thickest of it and while many who went in side by side with me whole hearted, brave soldiers, who had stood by me in many dangers, were left bleeding and mangled on the ground." Wilkin became isolated and had to fight his way out, only barely escaping capture when his horse bolted. He later wrote, "I think nothing of charging against equal numbers, but to charge into a whole army of cavalry and infantry and artillery and see your comrades mowed down by their sabres and the deadly fire of their musketry and cannon, is not particularly funny" (Wilkin letters). Pvt Alfred G. Ryder, Co. H, 1st Michigan Cavalry, was captured during the melee and later recorded in his diary, "I was taken prisoner in the terrific charge made by our regiment on the rebel hosts. 2 of my comrades are with me" (Ryder diary).

Thundering through clouds of dust behind Harman's troopers galloped the 7th Virginia Cavalry which veered to the right and charged at the flank of the 4th New York Cavalry, which Capt Myers reported as being "about 800 yards from the first line … we cut off a large number of them on our right, a portion of whom the Seventh captured and the others the Second and Twelfth [Virginia]" (*OR* I, XII, 2: 752). According to one of his troopers, "The line in blue appeared to vanish, for it scattered in all directions, the most of the enemy escaping through the woods skirting Bull Run" (quoted in Hennessy 1999: 434). Of these closing stages in the fight Pvt Fay, 7th Virginia Cavalry, wrote:

> We pursued them hotly and made a number of prisoners. In the pines on the low grounds approaching Bull Run I overtook and disarmed one of the 4th New York. After exchanging horses with him against his earnest protest that he would be shot if he went unguarded to the rear, I started my prisoner back and went on in the charge … (Fay 1915: 264)

The 4th New York Cavalry sustained three killed, including 2/Lt Jaques More (Co. G), five wounded, and 39 captured, one of whom was also wounded. Most of the prisoners of war from this regiment were paroled at Gainesville two days later. Unimpressed by the performance of the 4th New York Cavalry, Buford wrote a year later, "It failed me awfully at Bull Run" (*OR* I, XII, 2: 274). The Virginians pursued Buford's routed troopers for approximately three-quarters of a mile across the Lewis Ford toward the Warrenton Turnpike. In his official report of the action, Stuart pointed out that the melee at the Lewis Ford "was of remarkably short duration" (*OR* I, XII, 2: 737). Coming under artillery fire and realizing that taking up a position in the rear of the Union army was not particularly wise, the Confederate cavalry decided to stop their pursuit short of the Turnpike, where the 1st Vermont Cavalry which had been held in reserve was posted to cover the Union retreat along the Turnpike.

Col Thornton F. Brodhead, commanding officer of the 1st Michigan Cavalry, was reportedly the last Union cavalryman on the battlefield. Although he could have escaped with the rest of his regiment, he attempted to rally Buford's routed brigade and in so doing became involved in hand-to-hand combat with Capt Lewis Harman, adjutant of the 12th Virginia Cavalry, who overcame him and demanded his surrender. When Brodhead refused, the Confederate shot and mortally wounded the Union colonel and rode off with his horse, saddle, pistols, and saber. Dying three days later, Brodhead received a deathbed brevet to brigadier general for his bravery at Lewis Ford. He also wrote a public letter berating the performance of Pope and McDowell at Second Bull Run/Manassas (Frye 1988: 11).

Col Thornton F. Brodhead commanded the 1st Michigan Cavalry at Lewis Ford on August 30, 1862, and was mortally wounded attempting to rally his troopers. He died several days later in captivity after writing to his family that he hoped from heaven he would see "the glorious old Flag wave again over the undivided Union" (quoted in Johnson 2007: 60). (Library of Congress LC-DIG-cwpb-04571)

Buckland Mills

October 19, 1863

BACKGROUND TO BATTLE

Following Pope's defeat at Second Bull Run/Manassas, Lincoln reluctantly reappointed McClellan to command but he was again dismissed on November 5, 1862, for not pursuing Lee's army with sufficient vigor and aggression after Antietam/Sharpsburg. Two days later Maj Gen Ambrose Burnside was given command of the Army of the Potomac but, after failure at Fredericksburg and the disastrous "Mud March" of January 1863, when a further offensive campaign came to nothing, his resignation was also accepted.

Meanwhile, during October 1862 J.E.B. Stuart conducted the second of his audacious circumnavigations of the Army of the Potomac. In what was

A Union cavalry commander throughout the Civil War, Maj Gen George Stoneman was appointed by Maj Gen Joseph Hooker to lead the Cavalry Corps in the Army of the Potomac following the reorganization in April 1863. Later the same year he became Chief of the Cavalry Bureau in Washington, DC. He also led several raids into Confederate territory, the last of which supported Sherman's campaign in the Carolinas. (*Miller's Photographic History*)

The 2nd New York Cavalry received this unique Tiffany & Co. embroidered standard bearing the likeness of Senator Ira Harris on December 5, 1861, at Arlington Heights near Washington, DC. The flag – financed by Judge Henry Davies, uncle to Col J. Mansfield Davies, the original regimental commander – includes the regiment's nickname, "Harris Light Cavalry," embroidered above the portrait and an inspirational slogan "In God is our Trust" embroidered below. The "Harris Light Cavalry" reportedly carried the standard throughout its entire service from December 1861 until mustered out in June 1865. Today only about half of the flag exists and it rests on top of a modern sheer fabric to approximate its original size. (Courtesy NYS Military Museum)

known as the Chambersburg Raid, he seized horses and supplies without gaining much military advantage during a 126-mile ride through Pennsylvania and Maryland. On December 26, Lee ordered Stuart on a further raid north of the Rappahannock River to "penetrate the enemy's rear, ascertain if possible his position & movements, & inflict upon him such damage as circumstances will permit" (quoted in Wert 2008: 195). Reaching almost as far north as Fairfax Courthouse, Stuart's troopers seized 250 prisoners plus horses, mules, and supplies. Tapping telegraph lines, his signalmen also intercepted messages

The Third Bunting-issue Army of Northern Virginia battle flag was received by the 5th North Carolina Cavalry (63rd Regiment, North Carolina Troops) soon after arrival in Virginia during May 1863 and would have been carried at Buckland Mills. Measuring approximately 48in square, it was of infantry size rather than the 30in-square battle flag proposed for cavalry in 1861. None of the latter was issued for reasons unknown. The grandchildren of Col Peter G. Evans, original commander of the regiment, donated the flag to the North Carolina Museum of History in 1916. (Courtesy North Carolina Museum of History)

Commanding the Confederate cavalry rearguard at Buckland Mills, Maj Gen J.E.B. Stuart cooperated with Maj Gen Fitzhugh Lee in order to lure the Union cavalry of Brig Gen Judson Kilpatrick into a trap at Buckland Mills on October 19, 1863. (Library of Congress LC-DIG-ppmsca-38003 – Liljenquist collection)

This drawing by Edwin Forbes shows the violent aftermath of a cavalry charge with men and horses strewn across the battlefield. Approximately 1 million horses and mules were killed in combat during the Civil War. A total of 1,500 animals died at Gettysburg, of which 881 belonged to Union forces while the Confederates lost 619. (Library of Congress LC-DIG-ppmsca-20758)

between Union commanders, and Stuart sent a personal telegram to Union Quartermaster General Montgomery C. Meigs requesting him to furnish better mules in future as those he had captured were "very inferior."

In the North, Lincoln next appointed Maj Gen Joseph Hooker in his quest for a war-winning commander. Hooker reorganized the army and planned a summer campaign which ultimately resulted in yet another Union defeat at Chancellorsville on May 1–6, 1863. However, Hooker was the first Northern general to understand the strategic value of a centralized cavalry corps and he appointed Maj Gen George Stoneman to lead it. No longer subject to orders from small infantry units, the new Cavalry Corps would emulate its Southern counterparts by undertaking raids into enemy territory, destroying supplies and gathering intelligence. Although the end result was tactically indecisive, the performance of Union cavalry at Brandy Station on June 9, 1863, indicated that it was beginning to realize its potential.

At Gettysburg during the following month two further major cavalry clashes occurred on the third day of battle following Stuart's return from

another raid into Pennsylvania. On what became known as the East Cavalry Field, Stuart attempted to get into the Federal rear but was thrown back by the cavalry of Custer and Gregg, with the former urging on his Michigan troopers with the battle cry "Come on, you Wolverines!" At the South Cavalry Field, near Big Round Top, Brig Gen Judson Kilpatrick's cavalry made a difficult mounted charge against infantry over terrain broken by boulders and stone walls, and was repulsed by the Alabamians and Texans of Hood's division.

Three months after its defeat at Gettysburg, the Army of Northern Virginia lay entrenched south of the Rapidan River, still licking its wounds. Meanwhile, the Army of the Potomac, under Maj Gen George G. Meade since July 1863, prepared winter quarters around Culpeper Court House. Toward the end of September, Lee went on the offensive again and attempted to flank Meade only to sustain a further defeat at Bristoe Station on October 14. Following this he withdrew southwest toward the Rappahannock River with a rearguard composed of the cavalry divisions of Maj Gen Wade Hampton and Maj Gen Fitzhugh Lee, under overall command of J.E.B. Stuart. Hampton's division rode through Gainesville toward Warrenton while Fitzhugh Lee went via Auburn. On the morning of October 19, Hampton's cavalry occupied the buildings in the small township of Buckland Mills using them as cover against the Federals who – sensing the possibility of a further victory – had advanced and occupied the heights northeast of Broad Run.

Artist Edwin Forbes produced this drawing of a Union cavalry charge near Brandy Station on June 9, 1863. Approximately 20,000 horsemen fought in this action which lasted more than 12 hours and was the first all-cavalry battle of the Civil War. At the height of the battle charges and countercharges were made for almost three hours. (Library of Congress – LC-DIG-ppmsca-22378)

MAP KEY

1 1000hrs (approx.): Hampton's cavalry occupy Buckland Mills in order to cover Lee's retreat after defeat at Bristoe Station five days before. Kilpatrick's Union cavalry advance and occupy the heights northeast of Broad Run.

2 1005hrs (approx.): A shell narrowly misses Custer and his staff as they survey Confederate positions on the opposite bank of Broad Run.

3 1010–1200hrs (approx.): Union artillery, plus sharpshooters, deploys in the hills at Cerro Gordo under Custer and Davies and shells Confederate positions in Buckland Mills for about two hours.

4 1015hrs (approx.): Robinson's brigade is deployed to the ford 1 mile below the town.

5 1030hrs (approx.): Stuart receives a dispatch from Fitzhugh Lee outlining a plan to lure Union troops into a trap. Stuart would feign retreat west along the Warrenton Turnpike. When the Federal troops followed, a cannon shot would be fired to signal the attack. Stuart would turn and charge while Lee would assault the Federal left flank. Stuart begins his withdrawal out of Buckland Mills at about 1200hrs.

6 1200–1300hrs (approx.): Kilpatrick crosses Broad Run and halts to feed and water his horses. He sends out scouts to look for Confederate flanking movements. Believing there is no threat Kilpatrick orders Brig Gen Henry E. Davies, Jr., to take his 1st Brigade and pursue Stuart.

7 1400hrs (approx.): Stuart's cavalry reach the other side of the ridge beyond New Baltimore. Out of sight of the Federals, they turn and dismount behind the Pond Mountains and Baldwin Ridge while awaiting the signal to attack.

8 1430hrs (approx.): Kilpatrick's scouts report that a large body of cavalry is approaching from the south. Establishing

that this is the enemy, Kilpatrick deploys Custer's 2nd Brigade to defend the bridge and sends a courier ordering Davies to withdraw and return to Buckland Mills.

9 1440hrs (approx.): Wickham's brigade (Fitzhugh Lee's division), led by Col Thomas H. Owen, is unexpectedly halted by Custer's brigade and cannon fire from Pennington's battery.

10 1440hrs (approx.): The sound of Federal cannon fire signals the beginning of Fitzhugh Lee's attack and Stuart orders Hampton's division to charge.

11 1445hrs (approx.): The 1st North Carolina Cavalry charges headlong into the 2nd New York Cavalry and the rest of the Union cavalry column breaks and flees.

12 1450hrs (approx.): The whole of Fitzhugh Lee's division attacks and forces Custer's brigade to retire across the bridge. Custer's headquarters wagon is captured. Kilpatrick sends Pvt Henry C. Myer, Co. C, 2nd New York Cavalry, to guide the remains of Davies' column across Broad Run.

13 1450hrs (approx.): As part of Hampton's division reaches Buckland Mills the Confederate troopers become disorganized and Lt Col Rufus Barringer is injured when his horse crashes against a building. Maj William H.H. Cowles takes command of the 1st North Carolina Cavalry.

14 1500hrs (approx.): Reaching the remains of Davies' scattered troopers, some of whom are attempting to make a stand, Pvt Myer leads them across Broad Run. Hampton's troopers pursue the Union cavalrymen until they reach the safety of the lines of I Corps at Hay Market.

15 1500hrs (approx.): Custer's brigade is chased along the road to Gainesville until it also reaches the advancing I Corps infantry.

Battlefield environment

The Buckland Mills battlefield was dissected by Broad Run, the waters of which flowed from north to southeast, and the Warrenton Turnpike which linked Gainesville in the northeast with Warrenton in the southwest. The Run was about 17yd wide in places, had high water and steep slopes, and could only be crossed via the bridge at Buckland or at one of three fords, the Buckland Mill Ford being a few hundred yards north of the bridge, and the Kingsley Mill Ford and an unnamed ford being situated about a half-mile and 1 mile respectively south of the bridge. Steep cliffs edged the Run as it made a hairpin turn about a mile west of Buckland Mills. The Turnpike served as the Federal axis of advance and retreat during the battle and ran through what was described in Plate VII of the *Official Atlas of the Civil War* as a "hilly but open and fine agricultural region." After crossing the Buckland Bridge this road was bounded on both sides by

cleared farm land which was fringed about one-third of a mile back by woods. The small township of Buckland Mills stood on the north side of the Turnpike on the southwest bank of the Run. One mile west of the bridge and intersecting the Turnpike near the small hamlet of New Baltimore was a low wooded ridge running in a north–south axis and extending about a half-mile north and one mile south for a total length of approximately 1.5 miles. A small tributary called South Run divided this high ground and emptied into Broad Run behind the house at the Buena Vista Farm. Overlooking the eastern bluffs of Broad Run on a series of five hills stood the Cerro Gordo Farm. Northeast of this a half-mile-wide ridge of open land extended between the Hay Market–Gainesville Turnpike and the north fork of Broad Run, and provided the scene for the closing stages of the battle (Fonzo 2008: 28).

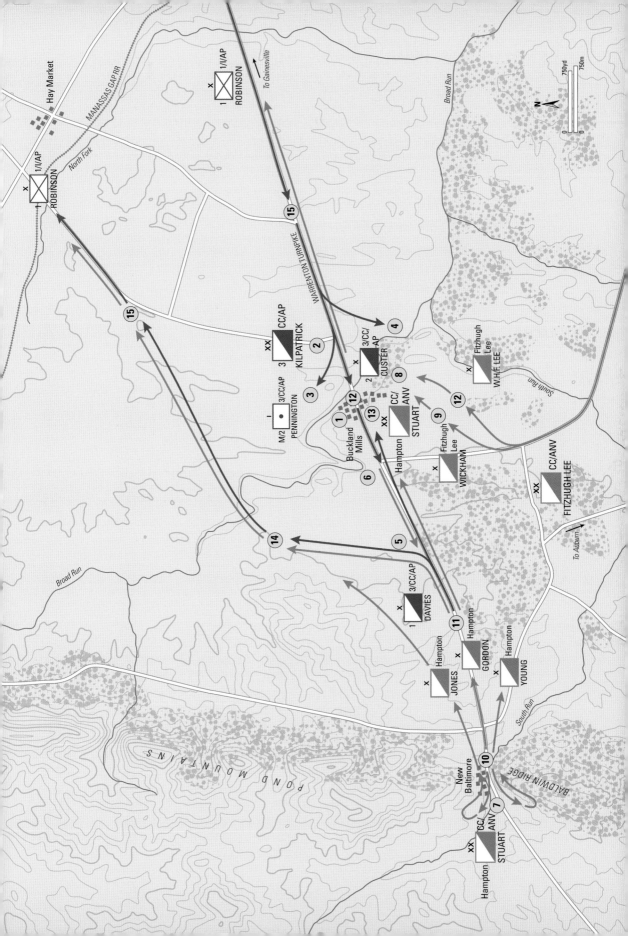

INTO COMBAT

Arriving with his staff and escort at the Buckland Mills Bridge at about 1000hrs, Brig Gen Custer halted in the road on the east bank of Broad Run to determine the situation. As he peered through his field glasses, he heard the boom of a cannon and seconds later a shell landed right in the midst of his party. Fortunately, no one was killed or seriously wounded and Custer hastily returned to the lines of his cavalry brigade. The battle of Buckland Mills, also known as "Buckland Races," was under way.

For approximately two hours Hampton's cavalry division, commanded by Maj Gen J.E.B. Stuart, held a position on the west side of the bridge, with artillery plus dismounted troopers serving as sharpshooters placed in the town, thwarting any attempt by the cavalry of Brig Gen Judson Kilpatrick to cross the river at that point. With immediate passage across Broad Run under his control, Stuart observed the Union force being deployed to threaten his flanks. Kilpatrick ordered part of Custer's Michigan brigade, with Battery M, 2nd US Artillery, commanded by 1/Lt Alexander C. Pennington, to occupy the hills at Cerro Gordo, while the remainder approached the ford 1 mile below the town. Meanwhile, Davies' brigade was massed in the woods along the eastern banks of the Run in preparation for an assault across the bridge.

Soon after Stuart began receiving fire from Kilpatrick's troops, a dispatch arrived from Fitzhugh Lee at Auburn stating that he was moving north to his support and suggesting a plan whereby the Confederates would give up their position in the town and control of the bridge, and feign retreat toward Warrenton. As Stuart withdrew along the Turnpike he would form up his troopers behind the wooded ridge west of Buckland ready for a counterattack. Once Kilpatrick had crossed over Broad Run to pursue him along the Turnpike, Fitzhugh Lee would swoop on the Federal rear and recapture the bridge, thereby cutting off their escape back across the river. A single cannon shot at the commencement of this attack would serve as a signal for Stuart to strike, thus forcing the Union cavalry back toward Fitzhugh Lee and catching them in a pincer movement.

Stuart began his withdrawal out of Buckland Mills at about 1200hrs. Of his movement across the river, Kilpatrick stated in his after-battle report:

> Having learned from scouts that no portion of the enemy was upon either flank, and that his entire force had passed to the south of Broad Run early that morning, I determined to cross the stream and ascertain, if possible, the strength and character of the enemy. After a determined effort of over two hours, General Custer had succeeded in pushing his command up to the bridge and on the hills to the right of the road overlooking the enemy's position. The Seventh Michigan had already crossed Broad Run at the [Buckland Mill] ford, and was moving down upon the enemy's flank with a strong line of skirmishers in advance. General Davies' brigade was massed on the left of the road, under cover of the woods, ready to cross. My whole command being now in readiness to cross, I ordered General Custer to charge the bridge. The charge was successfully made, the buildings upon the opposite side were gained and held by our sharpshooters, and in a few minutes General Custer's entire brigade had crossed, and the enemy was rapidly retiring in the direction of New Baltimore. (OR I, XXIX, 1: 382)

Based on a drawing by Alfred Waud entitled "Buckland from Mrs. Hunton's house," this *Harper's Weekly* engraving shows Battery M, 2nd US Artillery, commanded by 1/Lt Alexander C. Pennington, firing across Broad Run during the opening stages of the battle. The accompanying report described Buckland Mills as consisting of "about two dozen houses, a woolen factory, and a dilapidated mill," which is seen at rear right. The Hunton family sheltered in their basement as the battle unfolded around them. (Author's collection)

Kilpatrick next halted his command for an hour while his troopers fed their horses, and scouting parties were sent out in the direction of Thoroughfare Gap and Auburn in search of possible Confederate flanking attacks. Believing there was no threat, he ordered Brig Gen Davies to pursue the Confederates along the Warrenton Turnpike. Each time Davies' force came within carbine range, Stuart retreated farther toward Warrenton, luring his pursuers into a trap. Of the Federal advance Stuart's adjutant, Capt William W. Blackford, commented, "It was a broad, straight turnpike road, and as far as the eye could reach their column of splendidly equipped cavalry came marching on with flags fluttering and arms glittering in the bright autumn sunshine" (Blackford 1945: 241).

Most of Stuart's troopers withdrawing from Buckland Mills were unaware of the Confederate plan and were puzzled by their commander's willingness to retreat without offering any real opposition. As the Union column continued to follow, Stuart deployed a line of skirmishers either side of the Turnpike but kept his main column moving slowly toward Warrenton. By about 1400hrs Stuart's cavalry began to reach the other side of the ridge beyond New Baltimore. Out of sight of the Federals, they were turned and ordered to dismount while awaiting the time to attack.

At about 1430hrs a report came in from one of Kilpatrick's scouting parties that a large body of cavalry was approaching from the direction of Auburn. Thinking that this might be his Reserve Brigade under Brig Gen Wesley Merritt, he sent a courier with instructions for Davies to halt. Sent out to establish the identity of the approaching troops, a company of the 7th Michigan Cavalry returned at the gallop to report that it was a column of enemy cavalry "but a mile off and approaching rapidly" (*OR* I, XXIX, 1: 383). Kilpatrick at once ordered off the whole of the 7th Michigan Cavalry to delay the enemy as long as possible, while the remainder of Custer's brigade was deployed to defend the bridge at Buckland. Another courier was sent ordering Davies to return to the bridge but it is unclear whether Davies received that message before Fitzhugh Lee's cannon shot signaled the beginning of the Confederate assault.

The spearhead of Fitzhugh Lee's flank attack consisted of Wickham's brigade, commanded by Col Thomas H. Owen, with Lt Col William R. Carter's 3rd Virginia Cavalry at its head. Once in range of the 7th Michigan Cavalry and surprised to find Custer's brigade in front of it, Carter's regiment charged to within 1,000yd of the bridge when it was halted by cannon fire from Pennington's battery in the woods on the opposite bank of Broad Run.

The son of a poor farmer in St. Lawrence County, New York State, Willard W. Glazier left home at a young age to make a living as a trapper on the Canadian border. By 18 years of age he had saved enough money to buy a horse and in 1859 rode to Albany, the state capital, where he enrolled at the State Normal School, today the University at Albany, with the intent of becoming a teacher. Forced to leave after running out of money, he acquired temporary teaching posts in rural Rensselaer County and periodically returned to college when he had enough cash.

At the beginning of the Civil War, Glazier joined the Union Army along with most of his college classmates plus two instructors. As he had a horse he enlisted as a private in Co. E, 2nd New York Cavalry, or Harris Light Cavalry, at Troy, New York, on August 6, 1861. He was appointed first sergeant on an unrecorded date and was commissioned second lieutenant on August 24, 1863. Captured at Buckland Mills on October 19, 1863, he was held at Libby Prison, in Richmond, Virginia, from October 23 until May 6, 1864. He was next transferred to Camp Oglethorpe, near Macon, Georgia, and thence to Camp Davidson, Savannah, about three months later. Arriving at the Jail Yard in Charleston, South Carolina, on September 12, six weeks later he was moved on to Camp Sorghum, near Columbia, on October 5, 1864, from where he escaped on November 26, only to be recaptured after 21 days on the run near Springfield, Georgia. Escaping again shortly after, he finally managed to make his way back to Albany with the help of several African Americans,

although news of his death had reached his family. As his term of service had expired, he re-enlisted for one year as a first lieutenant in Co. L, 26th New York Cavalry on March 25, 1865, and was finally mustered out as a brevet captain at Ogdensburgh, New York, on July 1, 1865. During the post-war years, he pursued a career as an explorer and adventure travel writer, and wrote numerous books about his Civil War experiences.

Taken from the frontispiece of one of his books relating his Civil War service, this engraving depicts the youthful Willard Glazier as a brevet captain. (*Three Years in the Federal Cavalry*, 1870)

Halted behind the wooded ridge with the 1st North Carolina Cavalry, Capt Blackford recalled, "We waited with breathless impatience the boom of Fitz Lee's cannon. Not seeing us, the enemy was just ascending the little rise behind which we were, not two hundred yards distant, when rapid firing of cannon in Lee's direction announced his attack, and at the same moment our two columns were let loose, and at them we went" (Blackford 1945: 241). According to 1/Lt Anthony:

> The middle of the afternoon was passing when a single gun was heard far to the Federal rear. In an instant a dozen bugles sounded the call "to saddle" and in a moment more every man was in line. The Brigade of [Brig Gen James B.] Gordon was this day in front and the "Old First" was in the lead and occupied the road. Of course, now, all understood the game, and that the shock would largely fall on this small regiment standing square in front of the Federals across an intervening plain, only a few hundred yards off, well drawn up in splendid array. (*CO* Mar 3, 1895: 4:5)

Sitting his horse on the right of the road, Stuart viewed the situation intently as the Federal column drew closer, with mounted skirmishers on either flank

Rufus Barringer, 1st North Carolina Cavalry

Born in Cabarrus County, North Carolina, in 1821, Rufus Barringer graduated from the University of North Carolina in 1842 and was a lawyer and legislator in the Whig party prior to the Civil War. When North Carolina seceded from the Union in May 1861, he supported his state even though he opposed secession, and recruited a cavalry company called the Cabarrus Rangers which was designated as Co. F, 1st North Carolina Cavalry (9th Regiment North Carolina State Troops), with Barringer elected as captain. This regiment performed picket and scouting duty under Stuart during the Peninsula Campaign, the Seven Days' Battles, Second Manassas and the Maryland Campaign in 1862. Barringer continued to command his company during the 1863 Gettysburg Campaign, and was severely wounded in the face at Brandy Station, an injury that took five months to heal. Promoted to major for his gallantry on August 26, 1863, he took command of the 1st North Carolina Cavalry with the rank of lieutenant colonel following the wounding of Col Thomas Ruffin at Bristoe Station five days prior to Buckland Mills.

Recovering from a fall from his horse during the charge on October 19, 1863, Barringer went on to become a brigadier general and was captured by Federal scouts near Namozine Church on April 3, 1865.

As his brother was a personal friend and former Congressional colleague of Abraham Lincoln, Barringer met the Northern president briefly and Lincoln wrote a note to Secretary of War Edwin M. Stanton requesting special treatment for him in captivity. Unfortunately this favor backfired. After Lincoln's assassination, Barringer fell under suspicion due to this meeting, and was repeatedly questioned regarding any role he may have played in the conspiracy. Consequently Barringer was not released from custody until several months after most other Confederate prisoners had been freed.

Rufus Barringer was photographed in 1861 as captain of the Cabarrus Rangers which became Co. F, 1st North Carolina Cavalry (9th Regiment North Carolina State Troops), the regiment he would command by October 1863. (Courtesy of Jay Barringer & Greg Mast)

evidently in readiness to charge. With not a moment to be lost, he called out quickly, "Now, Gordon, is your time!" (quoted in Clark 1901: 458). Gordon turned to Lt Col Rufus Barringer and ordered him to "Charge with the First North Carolina!" followed by "charge that Yankee line and break it" (quoted in Clark 1901: 458). Accompanied by Chief Bugler Henry Litaker, Barringer next cantered his horse "Black Shot" to the head of his regiment, which by that time consisted of only about 200 officers and men. Meanwhile with the ease of trained veterans, the Virginians of Jones' brigade, under Brig Gen Thomas L. Rosser, deployed in column on the left of the road, while Brig Gen Pierce M.B. Young's brigade of South Carolinians and Georgians formed up on the right. The remaining three North Carolinian regiments of Gordon's brigade fell in behind Barringer's troopers with the 2nd North Carolina Cavalry next in the column. Riding near Barringer, Maj Cowles recollected:

> The response from the regiment, as it rushed forward, was that wild, unearthly, untrained, undisciplined, yet to the enemy terrific and terrible, Confederate yell, which swelled and grew as it passed from front to rear of our entire column. Down

from the crest of that ridge the regiment poured like an avalanche. With flashing sabres and the impetuous speed of a war-horse, nothing could withstand it. (Quoted in Clark 1901: 458)

Of the next few seconds, Lt Col Barringer recollected:

In a few moments more the whole command were down upon the Federals with drawn sabers ... the whole line emptied their pistols and carbines upon our devoted heads, and then deliberately wheeled about and galloped off. The volley, of course, checked our speed and produced some confusion all through our advanced lines. But in an instant more the charge was again sounded and the pursuit continued. (*CO* Jan 6, 1895: 4:4)

19-year-old 2/Lt Willard W. Glazier of Co. E, 2nd New York Cavalry, described the impact on the Union troopers:

The onset was terrible and we were taken completely by surprise ... The Harris Light [Cavalry], having been in front while advancing, by this sudden evolution was thrown in the rear, and was thus compelled to meet the desperate charges of the enemy in pursuit. Reaching *a little rise of ground in the road*, we made a stand, and for some time checked the advancing Rebels, by pouring into their ranks deadly volleys from our carbines and revolvers. (Glazier 1875: 324–25)

Offering a somewhat different interpretation, 1/Lt Anthony, 1st North Carolina Cavalry, observed that "instead of meeting the shock with a counter-charge, the Federals resorted to the pistol and carbine, and fired too quick, nearly every shot passing over the Confederates" (*CO* Mar 3, 1895: 4:5 & 4:6). All three Union troopers killed in this initial clash belonged to Co. I, 2nd New York Cavalry, which suggests they were near the front of the Union column and bore the brunt of the attack. In the 1st North Carolina Cavalry, 2/Lt William G. Grady was killed and two enlisted men were wounded, all coincidentally from Co. I, indicating that company may have led the charge.

Some of the 2nd New York Cavalry attempted to fight a rearguard action. 1/Lt Anthony remarked on the resistance offered by some of the Federal troopers, stating that "only the front squadron ... manfully held the road and for miles alternately reformed, coolly delivered a fire and again retreated" (*CO* Mar 3, 1895: 4:6). Maj Cowles continued:

But it was all in vain; panic seized them; the cohesion of their drill, discipline and organization was for the time destroyed, and individual effort amounted to nothing; break they must, and break they did. And yet, every time we ran into them they fought like brave men, and I verily believe that if we had given them two minutes more before taking the start we would have had the fight of our lives for the possession of that road. As it was, the front wavered, their column melted and broke, and though they made frequent rallies and attempts to reform, we gave them no time. Sabres and pistols were freely used by both sides in the melees which followed every time they were attacked from the rear. (Quoted in Clark 1901: 458)

Entitled "The Capture – Cavalry Fight at Buckland Mills," this wood engraving by J. Hoey and D.R. Fay depicts the 1st North Carolina Cavalry surprising and overrunning the 2nd New York Cavalry, also known as the Harris Light Cavalry, at Buckland Mills, Virginia, on October 19, 1863. Shown at center is 2/Lt Willard W. Glazier, whose horse was shot from under him, shortly after which he was trampled, knocked unconscious, and captured. (*Three Years in the Federal Cavalry*, 1870)

Most of the Union cavalry farther back in the column simply broke and fled and a running battle ensued as they were chased by the Confederates for nearly 8 miles. According to 1/Lt Anthony, the North Carolinians "again and again dashed into the very ranks of the flying enemy." The speed of Col Barringer's horse was so great that it "twice led him into the rear of the Yankees, but so complete was the panic that he escaped unhurt" (*CO* Mar 3, 1895: 4:6). According to Pvt Paul Means of the Mecklenburg Rangers (Co. F), 5th North Carolina Cavalry, Gordon's troopers "pursued them relentlessly, and almost resistlessly, the horses at full speed the whole distance" (quoted in Harrell 2004: 211). At one point, the 18th Pennsylvania Cavalry was "ridden down by its own cavalry" (Harrell 2004: 211) as the slower horses were pushed to one side by the fleeter mounts. As a consequence, elements of this regiment were also forced to turn and offer some resistance.

Farther back in the scattering Union column, Brig Gen Davies tried in vain to rally his troopers. Many of those galloping back toward Broad Run ran into the flank attack and many did not make it back across the river. By this time, Fitzhugh Lee had ordered up Brig Gen Lunsford L. Lomax's brigade and, assembling his whole division by about 1450hrs, launched an assault composed of both mounted and dismounted cavalrymen. This forced Custer to retire, with some of his troopers escaping across the bridge while others retreated along the river bank and crossed at the Buckland Mill Ford. Detailed as a clerk on Kilpatrick's staff and serving as a courier in the field, 19-year-old Pvt Henry Coddington Myer, alias Meyer, Co. C, 2nd New York Cavalry, experienced the flank attack near the Buckland Bridge as Fitzhugh Lee's division smashed into the Federals from the south:

> We had been driving the enemy during the morning toward Warrenton, and had halted to feed when a force of the enemy came unexpectedly in between Custer's and Davies's brigades, overwhelmed Custer's command, and drove it back across Broad Run; and *by taking possession of the bridge and the Warrenton pike*, had cut off General Davies's command … (Meyer 1911: 65)

Riding behind Brig Gen Kilpatrick as he withdrew with his staff toward the Buckland Bridge, Pvt Myer recalled that his brigade commander tried sending

Buckland Races

Seen through the eyes of a Confederate trooper, the 1st North Carolina Cavalry are depicted here at the moment they crashed into the head of the Union column and delivered "the deadly shock" of the cavalry charge near Buckland Mills on October 19, 1863. In what was considered in the South one of the most decisive Confederate cavalry victories of the Civil War, the surprised Union troopers commanded by Brig Gen Henry E. Davies, Jr., turned and fled back across Broad Run as far as Hay Market where they eventually found protection behind the lines of the Union infantry. The North Carolinians are clad mostly in civilian attire while an officer wears a military overcoat. Several others wear captured Union trousers and high boots with knee flaps. They are armed with M1840 sabers and a mixture of Colt Navy revolvers, single-shot percussion pistols, carbines, and muskets. Their horses are equipped with Richmond-issue Jenifer saddles over wool or Spanish moss saddle blankets. The enlisted man at bottom left has an arsenal-made three-buckle bridle and single-ring halter, while the officer has a captured 1859-pattern bridle and halter. The Union troopers of Companies E and I, 2nd New York Cavalry, many of whom are new recruits, wear infantry overcoats and sack coats. Headgear consists of 1859- and 1861-pattern forage caps and civilian brimmed hats. They defend themselves as best they can with Sharps carbines, Colt Army revolvers and M1860 Light Cavalry sabers. Some of them would attempt to make a further stand while being chased back toward Buckland Mills. Their horses are well equipped with McClellan saddles and bridles, and issue wool blankets. Also wearing an enlisted man's overcoat with an officer's dress hat, 2/Lt Willard Glazier (Co. E) is falling with his stricken horse, following which he was trampled, knocked unconscious, and captured.

"one or two staff-officers" to Davies with orders for him to fall back and join forces with Custer, but they failed to get through. Myer recalled that as Kilpatrick crossed the bridge with the rear of Custer's brigade

> [he] turned to me, as I was riding near him, no staff-officer being at the moment about, and remarked: "Meyer, somebody must get to Davies and let him know that Custer has been driven across Broad Run and that the enemy have got this bridge." On turning my horse to go back, he called out: "Tell him to make his way the best he can to Haymarket [*sic*] where he will find [Major] General [John] Newton's [I] corps." (Meyer 1911: 66)

Unable to return across the bridge as the Confederates were approaching the other end of it and were also moving along the bank so as to intercept Davies' men, Myer rode toward the Buckland Mill Ford in hopes of crossing there. His narrative continued:

> Riding until beyond their line I saw some of Custer's men, who had been cut off, come out of the woods at that point and cross the stream to escape, when I took advantage of the confusion to cross to the west side, trusting I would not be noticed and that the woods at that point would screen me from observation. (Meyer 1911: 66–67)

Meanwhile, Stuart's troopers continued to harry and chase the remains of Davies' brigade toward Buckland, but not all went well for the Confederates as their charge lost momentum and became somewhat disorganized. Many of the troopers of the 1st North Carolina Cavalry with the fastest horses kept up the chase, and these were joined by riders from the other regiments in Gordon's brigade which became mixed with the lead regiment. Others lagged behind and even dropped out of the chase as their less-fit mounts became winded or lame. As most of the Union cavalrymen escaped headlong to the rear, Young's brigade were charging through the woods on the right of the pike in an effort to hit them in the flank, but the Federal cavalry fled so rapidly, the Georgians never got into the battle. Still trying to lead the way, Maj Cowles recollected:

> As we approached [Buckland Mills] … our column became somewhat scattered, the fleetest horses outstripping others, and the capture by us of such as would break away from the enemy's crowded column contributed to this. At this point Major [*sic*] Barringer's horse became unmanageable. Breaking, or disregarding his curb, he rushed past everything, and as he entered the town, in the effort to stop him, he was thrown against a house with great violence, knocking the horse completely over and down and striking the Major against the house with such force as to cause serious injury to his arm and head, disabling him from further participation in the action. This placed me in command of the regiment. (Quoted in Clark 1901: 458–59)

In the meantime, Pvt Myer approached Davies' routed column as best he could:

> Being familiar with the country [based on campaigning in the same area in 1862], I made my way around their flank and rear, having the sound of Davies's firing to direct me to his whereabouts. I soon reached him and found him hard pressed. When I reported the situation, his men were rallied for another charge, which was led by Captain J.[ohn] F.B. Mitchell, [Co. C, 2nd New York Cavalry] so as to gain time to permit a withdrawal, as directed. We then galloped across the country, the forces opposing following on our flanks, until we crossed Broad Run farther up towards Haymarket [*sic*]. (Meyer 1911: 66–67)

Of this point in the action, Davies made no mention of Myer's help and stated:

> I sent forward my wagons, artillery, and the rest of my column to the left, with instructions to cross Broad Run and make toward Hay Market, and then, with the First [West] Virginia Cavalry and the Second New York, attacked and drove back the rebel cavalry that were charging my rear. This done, I ordered the whole command across Broad Run, and moved through the fields and woods toward Hay Market. (*OR* I, XXIX, 1: 387)

21-year-old Daniel Wight enlisted for three years as a private in Co. F, 5th New York Cavalry (First Ira Harris Guard) on September 12, 1861, and was present at Buckland Mills in 1863 when his regiment was involved in the defeat and hasty retreat of the Union column attacked by Stuart's cavalry. He re-enlisted on February 11, 1864, and was captured at Ream's Station on June 29, 1864. He died in a Confederate hospital in Columbia, South Carolina, on July 20, 1864. (Courtesy NYS Military Museum)

Back at Buckland Mills, Custer's brigade withdrew along the road to Gainesville and toward the advancing infantry of Maj Gen John Newton's I Corps. Kilpatrick's artillery was conducted away in safety under the guidance of Doctor Henry Capehart, surgeon of the 1st West Virginia Cavalry, who knew the country well. However, in the ensuing panic the "Boy General" was unable to save his headquarters wagons, baggage, and papers, most of which were captured by elements of the 1st and 2nd North Carolina Cavalry led by Maj Cowles. Custer continued to be pursued by Fitzhugh Lee's Virginians until his exhausted and demoralized troopers rode through the ranks of the Union infantry pickets to safety. Farther north, Davies' shattered brigade continued making its way across open country to the Hay Market Road after fording Broad Run and its North Fork with some of Stuart's cavalry still hot on their heels. These troopers also did not stop until they had reached the I Corps pickets at Hay Market, the total distance they covered being about 5 miles. Both Davies' and Custer's brigades re-formed once they reached Union lines. After the battle, Stuart fell back rapidly toward Warrenton and when the Federal cavalry advanced again cautiously, they found no enemy to oppose their occupation of the town.

Tom's Brook

October 9, 1864

BACKGROUND TO BATTLE

Promoted to lieutenant general and given command of all Union armies at the beginning of 1864, Ulysses S. Grant understood the concept of total warfare and believed, along with President Abraham Lincoln and Maj Gen William T. Sherman, that only the complete defeat of the Confederacy, and

Custer's division retires from Mount Jackson in the Shenandoah Valley on October 7, 1864, during "the Burning." Sitting his horse in the bottom right-hand corner, the "Boy General" watches as his troopers ride off in "column by fours." Several burning barns can be seen in the distance while dismounted skirmishers hold infuriated Confederate cavalry at bay. (Author's collection)

the utter destruction of its economic base via a scorched-earth policy, would bring an end to the Civil War. The Shenandoah Valley became a particular point of focus for this ruthless approach to the struggle. Known as "the breadbasket of the Confederacy," its farmers raised crops, cattle, and hogs which fed the Southern armies while its location was regarded as a back door for Confederate raids into Maryland, Washington, and Pennsylvania.

During the last Confederate invasion of the North, which occurred in July 1864, Lt Gen Jubal A. Early's II Corps, Army of Northern Virginia, invaded Maryland via the Valley and threatened the defenses of Washington, DC before being repulsed by the Union VI Corps, which was especially recalled from the front to deal with the emergency. As a result, Union cavalry commander Philip Sheridan was sent to drive Early's troops from the Shenandoah Valley and was advised by Grant, "Do all the damage to railroads and crops you can. Carry off stock of all descriptions … so as to prevent further planting. If the war is to last another year we want the Shenandoah Valley to remain a barren waste" (Sheridan 1888: I.486). Thus, during the fall of that year, the Army of the Shenandoah fought a series of battles under Sheridan which culminated in Union victories at Third Winchester and Fisher's Hill on September 19 and 21–22, 1864.

As Early's shattered forces retreated, Sheridan advanced almost as far south as Staunton, in Augusta County. Overextending his supply lines, which had to be hauled almost 100 miles by wagon, he decided to withdraw north to Strasburg on October 5 and on the way destroyed the agricultural potential of the Valley. In what was called "the Burning" by the local population, Sheridan's troops destroyed crops, barns, and mills during their 30-mile withdrawal. The division under Merritt withdrew along the Valley Turnpike while Custer's division took a roughly parallel course along the Back Road. Along the way the Union troopers also slaughtered herds of animals or drove them away, and liberated hundreds of slaves who would have been required to plant the spring crop of 1865. This aroused hatred and fury in the hearts of all Virginians. After only a few days the enthusiastic Union army had burned over 2,000 properties, turning hundreds of civilians into refugees.

Observing that Sheridan had begun a withdrawal back down the Valley, Early reorganized his force and determined to follow after him, and was joined by Brig Gen Thomas L. Rosser who arrived from Petersburg with the Laurel Brigade to take command of the wounded Fitzhugh Lee's cavalry division of about 2,500 men. Hailed by the local populace as the "Savior of the Valley," Rosser was determined to harass the Federals and reap revenge for their "barn-burning" atrocities. Containing many men from the Shenandoah Valley, his brigade consisted of the 7th, 11th, and 12th Virginia Cavalry, and the 35th Battalion Virginia Cavalry, also known as "the Comanches." Early's

Appointed to command the Middle Military Division on August 6, 1864, which encompassed the Shenandoah Valley, Maj Gen Philip Sheridan was ordered to destroy the food-producing capability of the area to help defeat the Confederacy. Known as the "burning," it infuriated Virginians. Confederate cavalry led by Maj Gen Thomas L. Rosser caught up with Sheridan's army on October 8, 1864, and fought the battle of Tom's Brook the next day. (Library of Congress LC-BH82-4012 B)

other, much smaller, cavalry division was commanded by Maj Gen Lunsford L. Lomax and consisted of approximately 800 men.

Keeping his infantry and artillery to the rear, Early sent his cavalry forward. Lomax's division was ordered to advance up the Valley Turnpike after Merritt's barn-burners while Rosser's division pursued Custer's division along the Back Road. As they advanced north, Rosser's troopers passed the smoldering ruins of farm houses which many of them had once called home. Commanding Co. A, 35th Battalion, Capt Franklin M. Myers recalled, "On every side, from mountain to mountain, the flames from all the barns, mills, grain and hay stacks, and in very many instances from dwellings, too, were blazing skyward, leaving a smoky trail of desolation …" (Myers 1871: 335). On several occasions during the next few days the Confederates attacked Custer's troops and drove them farther north. At noon on October 8, Rosser's advanced guard consisting of the 7th Virginia Cavalry again caught up with Custer's cavalry and, after a running fight, chased them across Tom's Brook. Meanwhile, Lomax's troopers arrived at Jordan Run, a tributary of Tom's Brook, and went into bivouac either side of the Valley Pike.

The Union forces on the north side of the river were deployed with Merritt's 3,500-strong cavalry division, under overall command of Brig Gen Alfred Torbert, encamped at the base of Round Hill. This prominent mound of wooded sandstone rose conspicuously 300ft above the Valley floor southwest of Strasburg, and a Union signal station stood upon it. Custer's division – two brigades, amounting to about 2,500 men – encamped on the north bank of Tumbling Run, northeast of Mount Olive. During the night of October 8, Rosser's troopers saw the numerous camp-fires of Torbert's cavalry spread out before them from their vantage point on Spiker's Hill, which revealed the greatly superior strength of Sheridan's mounted force.

In the Federal camp Sheridan was furious with the way his troopers had been harried during the past few days. In a meeting with Torbert, Sheridan

Sketched in pencil and Chinese white, this drawing by Alfred R. Waud depicts Brig Gen George Armstrong Custer saluting his West Point classmate Maj Gen Thomas L. Rosser minutes before the commencement of the battle of Tom's Brook on October 9, 1864. Of this incident, *Frank Leslie's* artist James E. Taylor recalled, "Out rode Custer from his staff on his handsome black mare, far in advance of his line, his glittering figure in plain view of both armies. Sweeping off his broad sombrero, he threw it down to his knee in a profound salute to his honorable foe. It was like the action of a Knight in the Lists!" (quoted in Gallagher 2006: 145). (Library of Congress LC-DIG-ppmsca-21069)

ordered him to "give Rosser a drubbing next morning or get whipped himself," adding that "the [Union] infantry would be halted until the affair was over," and informing him that he "proposed to ride out to Round Top Mountain [Round Hill] to see the fight" (Sheridan 1888: II.56.) Torbert formulated a simple battle plan for the next day. He would send an overwhelming force under Custer along the Back Road against Rosser's division while holding Lomax's troops at bay on the Valley Pike. Custer was to communicate with Merritt so the two forces could coordinate their advance.

Brig Gen Thomas L. Rosser was known as the "Savior of the Valley" when he arrived to reinforce the corps of Lt Gen Jubal A. Early with the Laurel Brigade at the beginning of October 1864. Placed in command of Fitzhugh Lee's division after the latter was wounded, Rosser pursued Sheridan's "barn-burning" cavalry with vigor as far as Tom's Brook where he was soundly defeated by a much larger Union force. When he heard about Rosser's misfortune after the battle, Early mockingly stated, "The laurel is a running vine" (quoted in McDonald 2002: 7). (*Miller's Photographic History*)

By the morning of October 9, 1864, Rosser's cavalry was deployed in a shallow arc behind stone fences and rudimentary breastworks on Spiker's Hill, with a reserve encamped a short distance farther south. A newspaper report in the Northern press stated, "The Rebels were advantageously posted on a commanding hill. Barricades and breastworks of rails and stones, contributed considerably to a position which was naturally formidable" (*PD* Oct 12, 1864: 3:6). Rosser placed Wickham's brigade, composed of about 800 men under Col Thomas Munford, on the left resting its right across the Back Road. Munford placed his troopers across the road with the 1st Virginia Cavalry on the extreme left and the 3rd Virginia Cavalry on the right, with the 2nd and 4th Virginia Cavalry in between. Farther south he posted a section of two guns under Capt John W. "Tuck" Carter, of Capt James W. Thomson's Virginia Horse Artillery, supported by Brig Gen William H.F. Payne's small brigade of about 300 men of the 5th, 6th, and 15th Virginia Cavalry. The right of his line, which extended to the Harrisville Road, was held by the Laurel Brigade under Col Robert H. Dulany. The 11th and 7th Virginia Cavalry occupied the left and center of the brigade line respectively, while the 12th Virginia Cavalry and 35th Battalion held the right. Skirmishers composed of dismounted elements of both the 11th Virginia Cavalry and 35th Battalion were posted in front of this line. Capt Franklin Myers stated that the men of the latter unit with carbines were sent to the front under command of 2/Lt Edward J. Chiswell, of Co. B, who, with "forty men, held a line more than a quarter of a mile in length …" (Myers 1871: 338–39). 2/Lt Chiswell would be wounded in the right thigh during the forthcoming Federal onslaught.

About 3 miles southeast of Rosser's position, Lomax's division was dismounted behind breastworks along Jordan Run. Described at the time as "very poorly armed and cannot properly be termed cavalry," very few had "any arms, except long Rifles [such as long-barreled "Kentucky" and Hawken rifles]" which could not be "handled on horse back for aiming." To make matters worse, they did not have sufficient ammunition "on hand to fire" (Gallagher 2006: 146).

MAP KEY

1 0600hrs: Custer's Third Division and Merritt's First Division, Army of West Virginia, advance along the Back Road and Valley Pike respectively toward the Confederate force at Tom's Brook.

2 0700hrs (approx.): After fording Tom's Brook, Merritt's division advances farther for a quarter-mile until its skirmishers make contact with Lomax's troops deployed below Jordan Run.

3 0710hrs (approx.): Some of Merritt's troops ride north to form a junction with Custer. Col Kidd's 1st Brigade rides toward the Back Road while Col Thomas C. Devin's 2nd Brigade veers left and approaches Tom's Brook along the Harrisville Road.

4 0715hrs (approx.): Col Pennington's 1st Brigade, Third Division is deployed in "line of battle" to launch a feint attack with the 18th Pennsylvania Cavalry and 5th New York Cavalry dismounted as skirmishers, and the 1st Vermont Cavalry and 1st New Hampshire Cavalry plus the brigades of Kidd and Devin mounted in reserve.

5 0715hrs (approx.): The batteries of Capt Charles H. Peirce, 2nd US Artillery, and Capt Dunbar R. Ransom, 3rd US Artillery, unlimber and open fire.

6 0715hrs (approx.): The 8th and 22nd New York Cavalry (2nd Brigade, Third Division) begin a circuitous route to attack the Confederate left flank on Spiker's Hill.

7 0720hrs (approx.): Some Union skirmishers fight their way across Tom's Brook.

8 0725hrs (approx.): The 35th Battalion and 12th Virginia Cavalry counterattack and drive the Union skirmishers back.

9 0730hrs (approx.): Aware that his flanking attack has begun, Custer orders a general advance shortly after which Merritt follows suit.

10 0735hrs (approx.): Capt William F. Dowdell, Co. C, 35th Battalion, leads a second countercharge which prevents the Confederate skirmishers from being cut off by the flank attack and enables them to escape.

11 0740hrs (approx.): The Confederate troops of both Rosser's and Lomax's divisions begin a panicky retreat which continues for over 20 miles and ends at Columbia Furnace and just beyond Woodstock.

Battlefield environment

The battlefield consisted of autumnal and undulating farmland and pasture, much of which was trampled and destroyed by almost constant troop movement during the past few years. This was dissected by Tom's Brook, a tributary of the winding Shenandoah River, which flowed diagonally from northwest to southeast. A smaller stream called Jordan Run joined the Brook farther south. Tom's Brook was forded in the northwest by the Back Road and in the southeast by the Valley Pike. The destroyed tracks of the Manassas Gap Railroad ran parallel with the Valley Pike and terminated south of Mount Jackson. The village of Tom's Brook sat either side of the river around the Pike. High ground called Spiker's Hill overlooked Tom's Brook

from the southwest. Below the river, the Back Road ran southwest along a partially wooded ridge toward Columbia Furnace. The smoking ruins of burnt-out barns dotted the landscape. The area is overlooked from the northwest by an approximately 3,000ft-high ridge collectively known as North Mountain and by the 1,100ft Round Hill from the east. An artilleryman serving one of the guns attached to Rosser's division, Cpl George M. Neese, recalled the weather on the day of the battle: "Rough fragments of dark wintry clouds came rolling over the North Mountain and scudded swiftly across the sky, now and then scattering a few snowflakes that were whirled through the crisp air by a chilly west wind" (Neese 1911: 322).

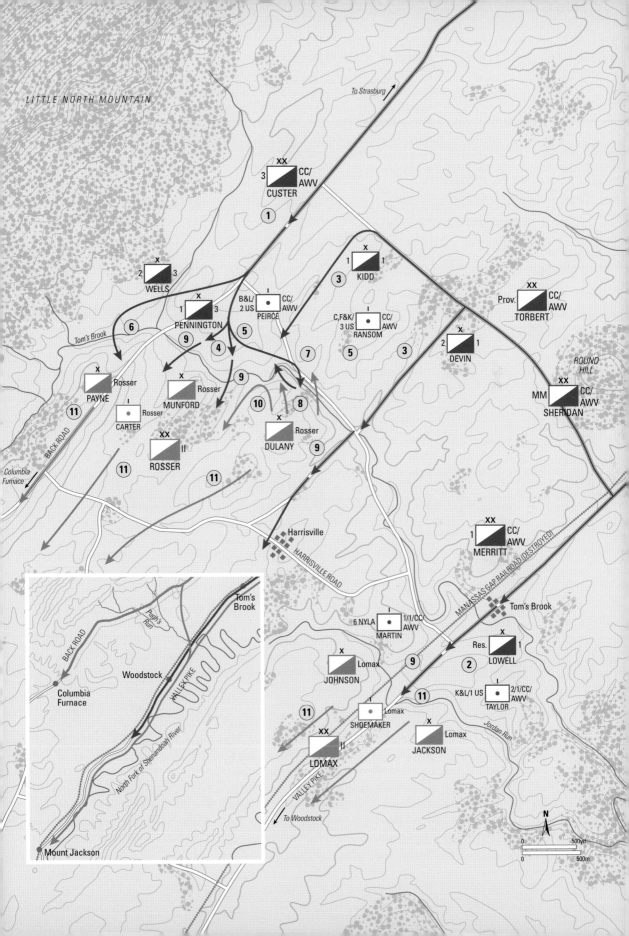

LITTLE NORTH MOUNTAIN

To Strasburg

XX
3   CC/
     AWV
CUSTER
①

X
1   1
     KIDD
③

XX
Prov.   CC/
         AWV
TORBERT

X
2   3
     WELLS

X
1   3
PENNINGTON

I
B&L/   CC/
2 US   AWV
     PEIRCE

⑥

⑨

⑤

I
C,F&K/   CC/
3 US   AWV
     RANSOM

X
2   1
     DEVIN

④

⑤   ③

ROUND
HILL

X
     Rosser
PAYNE

⑨

X
     Rosser
MUNFORD

⑨

⑩   ⑧

X
     Rosser
DULANY

XX
MM   CC/
      AWV
SHERIDAN

⑪

I
     Rosser
CARTER

⑦

XX
II
ROSSER

⑪

⑨

⑪

Harrisville

HARRISVILLE ROAD

BACK ROAD

Columbia
Furnace

XX
1   CC/
          AWV
MERRITT

Tom's Brook

I
6 NYLA   1/1/CC/
          AWV
MARTIN

X
     Lomax
JOHNSON

⑨

X
Res.   1
     LOWELL

②

I
K&L/1 US   2/1/CC/
            AWV
TAYLOR

⑪

I
     Lomax
SHOEMAKER

⑪

XX
II
LOMAX

X
     Lomax
JACKSON

Jordan Run

Tom's Brook

Pugh's Run

BACK ROAD

Woodstock

VALLEY PIKE

Columbia
Furnace

North Fork of Shenandoah River

To Woodstock

VALLEY PIKE

Mount Jackson

MANASSAS GAP RAILROAD (DESTROYED)

N

0   500yd
0   500m

INTO COMBAT

At 0600hrs on October 9, Custer's division advanced from its encampment at Tumbling Run near Mount Olive along the Back Road toward Tom's Brook. Merritt's division moved forward at the same time on the Valley Turnpike. Crossing Tom's Brook, Merritt's division advanced a quarter-mile until it made contact with Lomax's skirmishers at about 0700hrs. While Lowell was thus engaged, Kidd's Michigan brigade, distinctive in their Custer-influenced red neckties, rode north along the road parallel with Tom's Brook to connect and cooperate with Custer. Devin's 2nd Brigade followed but veered left and advanced either side of the Harrisville Road, linking up with the force on the Valley Pike and at the same time extending a skirmish line to connect with Kidd's brigade. As Custer's division trotted toward Rosser's lines, his 1st Brigade, commanded by Brig Gen Alexander C.M. Pennington, led the way with the 5th New York Cavalry at its head.

Meanwhile, the Confederates watched the mass deployment of Union troops in awe. Becoming alarmed, Munford sent several couriers to the bivouac in rear of his lines before Rosser came to see the situation at first hand. When Rosser finally arrived at about 0715hrs he was informed that his small force could not possibly hold their position "against such odds." Rosser responded, "I'll drive them into Strasburg by ten o'clock," prompting Munford to warn that the Confederate flank was "in the air" and could be turned, to which Rosser replied, "I'll look out for that" (quoted in Gallagher 2006: 143).

Sitting his horse on the Back Road atop Spiker's Hill, Rosser peered at the advancing blue tide through his field glasses, and soon spied his West Point classmate Custer riding out in front of the Union battle line. At about the same time, the "Boy General" scanned the Confederate lines and recognized his old friend and rival. Rosser later recollected that Custer wheeled his horse around and "gallantly raised his hat and made … a profound bow." In response Rosser turned to his staff and exclaimed that he intended to give his adversary "the best whipping today that he ever got!" (quoted in Hutton 1992: 86).

With formalities over, Custer proceeded to deploy his division. Realizing that he outnumbered Rosser, he extended his line westward by sending a force around to the northwest slope of Spiker's Hill to attack the Confederate left flank. If this was discovered by the Confederates they would be forced to abandon their position or extend their own line to prevent the Federals from flanking them. By attempting to defend more ground with his small division, Rosser would necessarily weaken his position elsewhere. If the Confederate commander did not discover this move, his flank would be taken by surprise and turned, making his entire position untenable. To ensure success, Custer arranged a diversionary attack at the Confederate front by sending forward a strong dismounted skirmish line behind which would advance the mounted 1st Vermont Cavalry and 1st New Hampshire Cavalry. The skirmish line consisted of the elements of the 18th Pennsylvania Cavalry on the right and 5th New York Cavalry on the left.

Following the command, "On right set – Deploy – Forward," each man dismounted, fastened his saber to his saddle, and advanced on foot with his seven-shot Spencer carbine while the horse holders withdrew the mounts to a safe distance. The horse artillery under Capt Charles H. Peirce, 2nd US Artillery, unlimbered on the hill in front of present-day St. Matthew's Church, while that of Capt Dunbar R. Ransom, 3rd US Artillery, did the same on high ground about a quarter-mile farther east, and both batteries engaged the Confederate artillery on Spiker's Hill. At the same time, the 8th and 22nd New York Cavalry, of Wells' brigade, led by Lt Col William H. Benjamin of the former regiment, took the difficult route through the woods and ravines in order to launch the flank attack up the northwest slope of Spiker's Hill.

Dealing with the Federal attack in his sector, Col Munford later recalled:

> The enemy, in considerable numbers, dismounted, were moving up to occupy the opposite bank … two full divisions – stretched from the Valley Pike, and connected entirely across to our front. As they developed I endeavored to keep my right extending, to prevent being turned. While I was thus engaged on the right, Rosser, superintending the left, became heavily engaged at the ford, and I was skirmishing with their dismounted men in front of me all along on the line of the creek bank. Rosser repulsed the first attack at the creek, which was intended as a feint, and his two guns under the gallant Carter were very active. (Munford 1885: 136–37)

Serving with Wickham's brigade, Capt William N. McDonald observed:

> The fighting began all along the front with little preliminary demonstration … A heavy line of [Federal] sharpshooters advanced, supported by numerous bodies of mounted men. Every opening disclosed moving masses of bluecoats, and soon they advanced, covering the hill slopes and blocking the roads with apparently countless squadrons … It needed but a glance at the oncoming foe to start Carter's guns to action. The intervening woods at first partly obscured them from view, but at every flash of blue through the trees, Carter sent a shot of defiance. The enemy's guns, greatly superior in number and admirably posted, now challenged his attention, and the Federal horse, taking advantage of this diversion, in dense swarms moved steadily forward. The sharpshooters on both sides were busy, those of the enemy pressing on with confidence. (McDonald 1907: 305–06)

Probing toward the Confederate line under heavy fire, some of the Union troopers managed to fight their way across Tom's Brook by about 0720hrs and sought cover on the opposite bank. In response to this onslaught, Rosser ordered the mounted troopers of the 35th Battalion and 12th Virginia Cavalry to charge, which temporarily halted the Union advance and pushed some of Pennington's dismounted troopers back across the water. 3/Sgt George W. Watson, Co. D, 12th Virginia, recalled:

> Their skirmishers were already firing at us. A spent ball struck me on the muscle of my right arm just as we started back. This stung but did not enter the skin. We had not gone one hundred yards when a horse was shot from under [Pvt] Onnie [Owen F.] Higgins, one of our company [,] and the horse fell on him. [Pvt] George Osbourn and I got off our horses and pulled him from under it. Helping him left us in the rear of our company … My horse kept jumping around so that I couldn't mount quickly. Osbourn was a few yards in front of me. The Yankees were coming in from the flank and they were just over the hill. I couldn't see them until I reached the hilltop for there was a fence on both sides of the [Harrisville] road. The first volley shot my horse. I went over his head as he fell on his knees and I came over

21-year-old Christopher C. Wenner enlisted "for the war" as a private in Co. A, 35th Battalion Virginia Cavalry, at Waterford, Virginia, on January 11, 1862. He was present with his command at Tom's Brook in 1864 and survived to be paroled at Harpers Ferry on April 18, 1865. Photographed soon after enlistment, he wears the uniform his company was probably originally provided with, which included an eight-button frock coat, and carries a saber. (Library of Congress LC-DIG-ppmsca-09866)

The charge of "the Comanches"

Confederate view: Troopers of the 35th Battalion Virginia Cavalry launched a counterattack across Tom's Brook, in the Shenandoah Valley, on the morning of October 9, 1864. Also known as "the Comanches" because of their wild riding and ear-piercing yells as they rode into battle, this unit was composed of about 200 Virginians, plus some exiled Marylanders, organized into six companies. Some of the former had been born and raised in the Valley and were infuriated by the barn-burning and destruction caused by Sheridan's cavalry. As with the rest of the Laurel Brigade, the men of this battalion carried a variety of arms, including Sharps carbines, Henry repeaters, Burnside carbines, Colt revolvers, and sabers — most of which had been captured from the enemy. The horses of the Laurel Brigade were described in an inspection report produced by their commander Maj Gen Thomas L. Rosser as "tolerably good," although on a divisional level they were assessed as being "in bad condition owing to the scarcity of forage" (Inspection Report Oct 18, 1864). The horse equipment includes a mixture of Richmond-issue Jenifer and captured McClellan saddles over Spanish moss blankets. Typically, the Confederate troopers wear a mixture of civilian clothing, having traveled light with few blankets or overcoats available to them. On the opposite bank of Tom's Brook can be seen the dismounted Union troopers of the 18th Pennsylvania Cavalry, with the 1st Vermont Cavalry and 1st New Hampshire Cavalry mounted in reserve in the rear. Some of the Federal troopers were driven back across the river at a cost of seven men of the Laurel Brigade killed or wounded.

Union view: Part of a feint attack to cover the main flanking movement of the 8th and 22nd New York Cavalry (Wells' brigade), the dismounted skirmishers of Companies D and E, 18th Pennsylvania Cavalry, reel back from the ferocity of the Confederate mounted counterattack. Only one Union trooper was wounded in this action, although those who crossed the river were driven back in confusion. The well-equipped Federals wear recently issued cavalry uniforms consisting of yellow-trimmed jackets and plain trousers with reinforced seats especially made for mounted service. They are without sabers which were an encumbrance when fighting dismounted and were fastened to their saddles, and make good use of seven-shot Spencer repeating carbines. Ammunition for the latter is carried in tin tubes held in elongated quick-loading cartridge boxes suspended from straps slung over their shoulders and held close to the body under their left arms. In the distance some of the troopers of the 35th Battalion Virginia Cavalry are seen charging across Tom's Brook in the face of the rapid Union fire. Minutes after this action, Wells' flanking attack commenced when Custer ordered a general charge which began the Confederate panic and retreat toward Woodstock and Columbia Furnace known in Federal ranks as "the Woodstock Races," and seen as revenge for what happened at Buckland Mills in 1863.

on my hands and feet. My horse did not get up while I was there. I jumped over a fence and hid in the weeds that were about three inches high. From the lay of the land they could not see me until they reached the top of the hill. I remained there until their company had passed with their equipment, artillery wagons, and etc. (Quoted in Kesterson 1993: 31–33)

Watson was captured later that day and spent the rest of the war in the prison camp at Point Lookout, Maryland. Close by during the same action, Col Dulany was severely wounded in the arm and Col Oliver Funsten, 11th Virginia Cavalry, assumed command of the Laurel Brigade. Elsewhere within the ranks, Pvt Isaac Anderson, Co. B, 12th Virginia Cavalry, was shot through the lungs and carried from the field, while 1/ Sgt Thomas S. Grubb, Co. A, 35th Battalion, was also seriously wounded and died a week later. Another two sergeants and one enlisted man in this unit received gunshot wounds.

As Custer regrouped his skirmishers, his flanking force under Lt Col Benjamin advanced in triple "column by fours" up the northwest slope of Spiker's Hill and into Rosser's left. Wheeling around, he pointed his saber at the Confederate line and at about 0730hrs bellowed, "Now go for it!" (Urwin 1983: 200). Farther south, Merritt's division attacked at about the same time and Devin's brigade drove a wedge between the two Confederate divisions. With Pennington's 1st Brigade (Third Division), Maj Phillips, 18th Pennsylvania Cavalry, recalled, "Soon the whole line was in motion and advanced as rapidly as the nature of the ground and the wearied conditions of my horses would allow, driving the enemy's skirmishers before it" (Publication Committee 1909: 111). With his regiment to the left of the 18th Pennsylvania Cavalry when the main Union mounted attack commenced, the Rev. Louis N. Boudrye, Chaplain of the 5th New York Cavalry, wrote:

> This was a pure cavalry fight, and one of the most spirited of the war. Having properly planted his artillery, and disposed his force as advantageously as possible, the general [Custer] ordered the bugles on the entire line to sound the advance, and leading the Fifth New York in person, he made a dash on the enemy's central position in the road. Our color bearer, Sergeant [John] Buckley, Company C, displayed his usual bravery, bearing our flag close by the side, and, at times, ahead of the general's. (Boudrye 1868: 178)

Riding at the head of Co. C, 2nd Ohio Cavalry, 2/Lt Luman H. Tenney stated briefly in his journal, "5th N.Y. in advance. 3rd N.J. [in] support. Line soon formed and advance sounded, then charged. Went in with 2nd Ohio" (Tenney 1914: 132).

As Benjamin's troopers charged into Rosser's left, the 12th Virginia Cavalry was driven back by the massed frontal attack on the right which isolated the Confederate skirmishers. According to Capt Myers, 35th Battalion, "Lieutenant Chiswell and his men had to make a run for it, barely escaping capture ..." (Myers 1871: 339). About this time, Capt William F. Dowdell, Co. C of the same unit, led another mounted countercharge which enabled most the Confederate skirmishers to escape. According to Myers:

A farmer's son born in 1848 in Troy Township, Pennsylvania, J. Andrew Wilt initially served in Co. A, 35th Pennsylvania Militia Infantry from July 2 to August 7, 1863, and was 16 years old when he enlisted as a private in Co. L, 18th Pennsylvania Cavalry (163rd Volunteers) on March 24, 1864, probably being appointed a bugler almost immediately. After Tom's Brook and the pursuit which followed, he served in that capacity with his company during the fighting at Cedar Creek. After the remnants of Early's army were captured at Waynesboro, Wilt helped escort about 1,500 Confederate prisoners to Winchester. Wilt was finally mustered out with Co. C of that regiment on October 31, 1865. He wears a rather oversized, dark-blue, full-dress cavalry jacket, and sky-blue kersey trousers, plus non-regulation brimmed hat with yellow cavalry cord and 1858-pattern militia-style crossed-sabers insignia attached to the crown. He holds a Model 1840 Dragoon saber. (*History of the Eighteenth Regiment of Cavalry*, 1909)

The son of Martha Carper, a wealthy farmer resident in Fairfax County, Virginia, 22-year-old Philip W. Carper enlisted "for the war" as a private in Co. A, 35th Battalion Virginia Cavalry, at White Post on December 17, 1862. Wounded and captured at Brandy Station on June 9, 1863, he was exchanged for a Union prisoner on June 26, 1863. Captured again in a skirmish at Broad River, Virginia, on December 27, 1863, he was transferred to the infamous Point Lookout Prison Camp in Maryland on February 3, 1864, and exchanged once more ten days later. Rejoining his battalion, he fought at Tom's Brook but managed to escape capture and was one of only about 80 men who continued to serve with his battalion throughout the Appomattox Campaign, following which he finally surrendered at Edwards Ferry, Maryland, on May 1, 1865. Photographed in 1862, Carper wears the plain gray uniform that White's Rebels (Co. A), 35th Battalion Virginia Cavalry, received soon after enlistment. His cap has crossed-sabers insignia with letter "A" above, and he holds an M1840 Heavy Cavalry saber. (Library of Congress LC-B8184-10018)

When the lines commenced to give way the artillery of Captain Thompson [*sic*] was firing rapidly upon the advancing columns of the enemy, and made desperate efforts to check the Yankees long enough to give Rosser a chance to rally his people, but nothing could bring anything like order out of the confused mass of fugitives that fled so wildly from the field. They had been flanked, and … gave way to a panic that increased each moment … (Myers 1871: 340)

Munford recalled, "We could now hear the yell of the column on our left and rear, and on my right we could hear Lomax's guns receding. I saw we had no possible chance now but to move out, and that, at a run, my left had given away, and it was only by a quick run that we escaped capture" (Munford 1884–85: 140). Capt Myers continued, "Every soldier knows that it only requires a shout in the rear to keep a stampeded force on the run, and it was so now, for the author saw fully six hundred veteran Confederate troops flying madly along the 'back road'" (Myers 1871: 340). Recalling how Rosser's cavalrymen abandoned their artillery and train to secure their own safety, Munford added, "It became more of a contest of speed than valor" (Munford 1884–85: 140). Thus, Munford's brigade headed for the rear in chaos, followed closely by Payne's troopers with the Laurel Brigade bringing up the rear. The action at Tom's Brook was over by about 0745hrs, and what would become known as "the Woodstock Races," as the Confederates dashed over 20 miles south to Woodstock and Columbia Furnace, had begun.

From his vantage point on Round Hill, Sheridan watched the unfolding action with delight and later recorded, "The result was a general smash-up of the entire Confederate line, the retreat quickly degenerating into a rout the like of which was never before seen. For twenty-six miles this wild stampede kept up, with our troopers close at the enemy's heels …" (Sheridan 1881: II.58). Brig Gen Torbert stated, "After a spirited engagement for about two hours, the enemy seeing that they were being flanked and severely pressed in front, gave way in great confusion, which was immediately taken advantage of by both division commanders" (*OR* I, XXXIII, 1: 431). Leading his regiment in the Union charge, Maj Phillips, 18th Pennsylvania Cavalry, recollected, "When the enemy's center gave way, the right of my line was quite far advanced and was in a position to give a flank fire as he began to retreat from the top of the hill, where his artillery was last in position" (Publication Committee 1909: 111). Encountering fences and ditches in his path, Phillips quickly ordered his chief bugler to sound "Rally on the Officer," following which he led his troopers over to the Back Road along which to continue the pursuit.

While most of Rosser's troopers fled southwestward along the Back Road, some took a side lane beyond Spiker's Hill through Saumsville toward Woodstock. As the Union cavalry followed Rosser's demoralized command, pockets of Confederates attempted to rally, but the overwhelming numbers of the Federal cavalry surrounded them within seconds. At the forefront of the chase, the 18th Pennsylvania Cavalry captured much of the Confederate wagon train. Having brought as many of his command together as possible, Maj Phillips pushed forward rapidly in pursuit, passing by the right flank of the artillery and entering the main road about 500 yards in rear of the wagon train … The enemy made a stand in the corner of a wood for a few minutes, killing [First] Lieutenant [John R.] Winters, who had emptied his pistol and was moving furiously upon them with drawn saber … the wagons were left to the mercy of any one who had a horse swift enough to overtake the terrified teamsters. (Publication Committee 1909: 111)

Both pieces of Thomson's artillery were also captured by the 18th Pennsylvania Cavalry. At about 0800hrs Munford attempted to rally his brigade and retake some of the captured wagon train. Joined by Rosser, who advised him that the rest of his command was forming to their rear, the two officers peered through the battle smoke and saw glimpses of what seemed like an entire Union regiment approaching with drawn sabers. Turning to his brigade commander Rosser shouted, "We can't do it," and girded himself for a further onslaught. Munford recalled:

> My sharpshooters engaged them, and we had another sharp skirmish in which Lieutenant Abner Hatcher, of Company A, Second Virginia, was killed, and we lost some others. We fell back under fire until we reached a body of timbers which afforded shelter for our men, after which the enemy retired, and we moved to Columbia Furnace, where the remnant of our division and our artillery, officers and men, had assembled. A more discomfited looking body I have never imagined. (Munford 1884–85: 137)

Meanwhile, Lomax's division was chased south toward Woodstock where it was joined by a confused portion of Rosser's command which had taken the side road. This force attempted to make another stand behind Pugh's Run but were soon scattered and the Union troopers pressed forward, driving the Confederates as far as Mount Jackson. On the Back Road, Custer's men followed Rosser and Munford about 19 miles to Columbia Furnace, where other remnants of the Laurel Brigade also rallied and made a stand, and the Union cavalry finally withdrew back up the Valley toward Strasburg. Along both routes many more exhausted Southerners had escaped into the woods and mountains.

The Confederate forces of Lomax and Rosser make a stand against Sheridan's cavalry in front of their hospital buildings at Woodstock following their retreat from Tom's Brook earlier that day. The accompanying report in *Frank Leslie's Illustrated* stated, "The struggle was a fierce one. Our men eager in pursuit, but the rebels beaten but desperate, and straining every nerve to save themselves from total disgrace, and ready to die to the last, to be able to carry off at least one gun." (Courtesy of the Anne S.K. Brown Military Collection)

Analysis

LEWIS FORD

When Brig Gen Robertson and Brig Gen Buford clashed at Lewis Ford on August 30, 1862, Southern horsemen were superior in every respect and basked in the success of Stuart's raids of June through July of that year. Nevertheless, there were signs that the cavalry under Buford, many of whom were new to combat, were beginning to master the art of mounted warfare. They stood their ground in the face of the initial charge of the 2nd Virginia Cavalry, and might have continued to give a good account of themselves had their commander eventually committed his whole brigade to combat. Completely overwhelmed by the ferocity of the charge of Robertson's brigade, they broke and ran across Lewis Ford and joined the rest of Pope's army in its flight to Washington, DC.

Both commands sustained significant casualties at Lewis Ford. Robertson had five men killed and 40 wounded, with Col Munford included in the latter. Buford's losses were significantly heavier with approximately 300 killed, wounded or captured, including Col Brodhead who bravely stood his ground. All of the Union staff officers had their horses shot out from under them. 1/Sgt Wilkin, 1st West Virginia Cavalry, lamented, "One Co.[mpany] in our brigade had only six men left after the fight. Our Co. lost only 9 men yet it was so much exposed, perhaps more exposed than any but O the destruction of life I witnessed on that awful day" (Wilkin letters). In his official report of the action, Stuart claimed, "Nothing could have equaled the splendor with which Robertson's regiments swept down upon a force greatly outnumbering them, thus successfully indicating a claim for courage and discipline equal to any cavalry in the world" (OR I, XII, 2: 737). In a letter to his wife Flora on September 4, 1862, Stuart confided, "We knocked Buford's Brigade into Bull Run, capturing 220, [&] killing a col.[onel]" (Stuart Papers Sep 4, 1862).

One Virginian cavalry officer involved in the fight reported in the Richmond press that the Union cavalry was "utterly demoralized and disorganized. They hurried along in great droves like frightened cattle, officers and men being mingled indiscriminately and inextricably. Our men followed them up and slaughtered them at leisure" (*RE* Sep 9, 1862: 1:2). To a certain extent Buford had mismanaged the cavalry under his command, only half of whom were committed to battle. However, his troopers had shown courage in their initial charge on the Confederates, and had for a short time covered the retreat of Pope's army before finally being routed by Stuart's more experienced troopers. In some respects, their performance augured well for what was to come as the cavalry of the Union Army gained further experience in combat.

BUCKLAND MILLS

Becoming known in the Confederate ranks as the "Buckland Races" because of the extent of the Union retreat and Confederate pursuit, the battle of Buckland Mills was viewed as a resounding victory in the South and went mostly unreported in Union dispatches and reports. After the indecisive result at Brandy Station that summer and subsequent criticism in the Southern press, J.E.B. Stuart relished this success. The Confederate commander declared that toward the end of the action he saw "the deplorable spectacle of 7,000 cavalry dashing hatless and panic-stricken through the ranks of the infantry" (*OR* I XXIX, 1: 452 quoting anon. Union writer). Meanwhile, Brig Gen Kilpatrick reported that the troopers of both Custer and Davies safely reached their "infantry supports at Gainesville and Hay Market, with their brigade organizations preserved" (*OR* I, XXIX, 1: 383). However, the honors of the day were not as unevenly divided as Stuart's exaggerated comment indicated, for the Confederates had the whole of their cavalry force in field, its strength being 6,867 troopers, while Kilpatrick's division numbered only about 3,500 men present for duty (*OWH* Oct 20, 1913: 10:3). Davies makes no

This cavalry jacket was worn by William H. Bettes who enlisted as a private in Co. L, 6th Ohio Cavalry on October 5, 1861. This regiment served in the Eastern Theater from May 1862 until the end of the Civil War. As Bettes was appointed and mustered in as a second lieutenant a month later, his enlisted man's jacket is in an excellent state of preservation as it was worn for only a short period of time. In use with US troops since 1833 and introduced with yellow trim for cavalry use in 1855, the jacket was fastened by 12 small cavalry "C" buttons in gilt and had two buttons of the same size on the cuffs. The 3in standing collar had two blind button holes each side which terminated in two more small buttons. The waist belt was supported by a buttoned flap on the left hip and two small loops of cloth at the bottom of the trim on the back seams. The jacket was preferred to the sack coat by many troopers and often worn in combat. (Courtesy of Dr. Michael Cunningham)

mention of the important role played by Pvt Henry Myer, 2nd New York Cavalry, in guiding elements of his shattered column to the safety of Union lines, which illustrates the difference between official reports and personal accounts.

Even so, Buckland Mills proved the worth of the classic cavalry charge which in this case was performed in triple "columns by fours," although the two flanking columns made much less impact than the North Carolinians galloping along the Warrenton Turnpike. Although Kilpatrick managed to prevent a complete disaster by posting Custer's brigade to defend the bridge crossing over Broad Run, which enabled some of his troopers to escape by that route, the action was an embarrassing humiliation. This was particularly so for Custer, whose headquarters wagon, containing clothes, official papers, and personal possessions, was captured. Furthermore, the troops Kilpatrick commanded were considered some of the best cavalry in the Army of the Potomac and they had been worsted in no uncertain terms. Total Union casualties amounted to 13 killed, 40 wounded, and 184 captured. Bearing the brunt of the initial Confederate charge and attempting to fight a rearguard action, the 2nd New York Cavalry lost the most men in Davies' brigade, sustaining four killed, three wounded, one missing, and 43 captured, which represented about one-seventh of the total regimental strength. In comparison the total Confederate command lost only nine killed, 29 wounded, and three captured, one of whom was also wounded.

After the battle, Pvt Means, 5th North Carolina Cavalry, stated that the Union troopers "fought stubbornly at first but nothing could resist the impetuous charges of the … North Carolinians and those boasting [Federal] columns broke in confusion" (quoted in Harrell 2004: 210). 1/Lt Whitmel Anthony commented, "Of all the regular mounted charges of the war this was probably the most complete in its success [,] the most daring … and the most glorious in its results" (*CO* Mar 3, 1895: 4:5). Illustrating the youthfulness and inexperience of some of the troopers involved at Buckland Mills, 17-year-old Pvt John P. McGinnis of the Mecklenburg Rangers (Co. C), 1st North Carolina Cavalry, wrote, "These were the first dead Yankees I saw. It was my first fight, as I had only been in the army three days" (*CO* Jan 10, 1902: 7:1).

TOM'S BROOK

The South's defeat at Tom's Brook on October 9, 1864, represented a massive reversal of fortune for Confederate cavalry which had mainly enjoyed success on the battlefields of the Eastern Theater of the Civil War since 1861. Seen as pure revenge in Union ranks for the humiliation of Buckland Mills, particularly by those under Custer's command, it was referred to as the "Woodstock Races" because some of Rosser's troopers, and most of those under Lomax, retreated in panic about 20 miles to the small township of Woodstock.

A scarcity of records makes it difficult to determine the number of Confederate casualties and captured in Rosser's command during this action. The campaigning of the previous few days made enumeration of the men involved in the action hard for officers to assess. Reluctant to record the extent of the disaster, Rosser did not produce an after-battle report and did not expect one from any of his subordinates. However, Lt Gen Jubal Early reported vaguely that the loss in killed and wounded in both Confederate cavalry divisions

combined was "less [than] 1,000," adding that in "the early part of the day it was not more than 100." Regarding captured, he could not give a figure but stated "I think very few. Many of the men scattered, and are still coming in" (*OR* I, XXXXIII, 1: 560). A Northern newspaper correspondent commented that there were "about four hundred [Confederate] prisoners" (*PI* Oct 13, 1864: 3:1). In his official report Sheridan stated:

> Merritt captured five pieces of artillery. Custer captured six pieces of artillery, with caissons, battery forge, &c. The two divisions captured thirty-seven wagons, ambulances, &c. Among the wagons captured are the headquarters wagons of Rosser, Lomax, and Wickham, and Colonel Pollard [Munford]. The number of prisoners captured will be about 330. (*OR* I, XXXXIII, 1: 31)

According to the report of Brig Gen Torbert, 270 of these were taken by the troopers of Custer's division. Regarding Union casualties, Torbert stated, "My losses in this engagement will not exceed 60 killed and wounded, which is astonishing when compared with the results" (*OR* I, XXXXIII, 1: 431). According to unofficial sources, the Confederates suffered approximately 20 killed, 50 wounded and 280 missing or captured, while the Federals sustained ten killed and 47 wounded. Several days after the battle, Sheridan exclaimed that it was "a square cavalry fight, in which the enemy was routed beyond my power to describe" (*PI* Oct 13, 1864: 1:1). In his after-battle report, Early stated:

> This is very distressing to me, and God knows I have done all in my power to avert the disasters which have befallen this command; but the fact is that the enemy's cavalry is so much superior to ours, both in numbers and equipment, and the country is so favorable to the operations of cavalry, that it is impossible for ours to compete with his. (*OR* I, XXXIII, 1: 559)

Although he was proclaimed as the "Savior of the Valley," this was Thomas Rosser's first battle as a divisional commander; his inexperience accounts to some extent for his lack of judgment and poor performance, but does not make allowances for his arrogance. Referring to the manner in which he defeated Rosser, Sheridan commented, "I deemed it best to make this delay of one day … and settle this new Cavalry General!" (*NYT* Oct 11, 1864: 4:3).

Produced in 1884 by William T. Trego and entitled "The Pursuit – Woodstock Races," this painting depicts Custer's cavalry pursuing Rosser's Confederate cavalry along the Back Road after Federal success during the battle of Tom's Brook. This painting was originally owned by Jerome Byron Wheeler, who served in the 6th New York Cavalry (2nd Brigade, First Division) during the battle. (Private collection – courtesy of the James A. Michener Art Museum)

Conclusion

Having learned well from earlier defeats, the Federals had by 1864 produced a mounted arm superior to that of the South in terms of equipment, organization, logistics, and leadership. They had achieved parity in battle on June 9, 1863, at Brandy Station, the largest predominantly mounted battle ever fought on the American continent, and at Yellow Tavern on May 11, 1864, where the outnumbered Confederate cavalry was defeated and J.E.B. Stuart was mortally wounded, robbing the South of its most effective cavalry commander. But it was not until October 9, 1864, at Tom's Brook, that the Union horseman at last completed the reversal of roles and fully worsted his Southern counterpart on the battlefield. The action at Tom's Brook and the large-scale use of dismounted skirmishers are evidence for the rise of the "hybrid cavalryman" who could fight just as effectively dismounted as he could on horseback once in possession of the Spencer carbine.

This change in fortune of equine military power was also due in part to the failing condition of the Confederate Ordnance Bureau. Defeats in 1863 at Vicksburg and Port Hudson in the west and Gettysburg in the east had been disastrous for the Confederacy which lost a total of approximately 70,000 small arms, plus a large number of cannon, ammunition, and accouterments, and substantial quantities of powder. Replacement of this material would take months, if it was possible at all. With the loss of the Mississippi River, which in particular had provided access to Texas cattle, leather for cavalry equipments was also in short supply. Blockade running was to prove the only remaining source for many of these items. On August 11, 1863, Maj Smith Stansbury, ordnance officer at the bureau's depot in Bermuda, pled with Maj Caleb Huse, CS purchasing agent in London: "We need immediately carbines (for cavalry), Revolvers (for cavalry), equipments (for cavalry), saddles, &c, &c." (Vandiver 1947: 80). A constant problem since 1862, the scarcity of horses was acute by the summer of 1864. Of the severely depleted cavalry of the Army of Northern Virginia, over a quarter

Born in Cumberland County, Pennsylvania, in 1846, Levi F. Hocker appears to have enlisted under age in Co. F, 17th Pennsylvania Cavalry on September 23, 1862. He was captured during the Shenandoah Valley on September 24, 1864, probably while carrying dispatches between Harpers Ferry and Martinsburg, and was paroled on February 28, 1865. He sits his horse in this quarter plate reversed tintype, and is a good example of a well-equipped enlisted man of the Union cavalry. He has removed his 44-caliber six-shot M1861 Remington revolver from its holster and tucked it into a carbine socket buckled to the "D" ring of the saddle's quarter straps. An M1860 Light Cavalry saber with leather sword knot has been transferred to his right hip to compensate for the reversed photographic process. His horse equipment includes a not-normally-issued breast-strap with circular brass breast plate, and crupper around the animal's tail, to prevent his McClellan saddle from slipping forward or back. A metal chain is attached to his animal's halter as a hitching strap. Normally associated with artillery halters, this possibly indicates a shortage of leather for cavalry equipment. (Library of Congress LC-DIG-ppmsca-33458 – Liljenquist collection)

were dismounted and locked in a debilitating struggle in the trenches around Petersburg and Richmond. Indeed, in a letter to President Jefferson Davis on July 5, 1864, Robert E. Lee stated: "The subject of recruiting and keeping up our cavalry force, has occupied much of my thoughts, especially since the opening of the present [Petersburg] campaign. The enemy is numerically superior to us in this arm, and possesses greater facilities for recruiting his horses and keeping them in serviceable condition." In conclusion he urged that on an increase in supply of horses, and recruiting cavalry "depends the issue of the campaign in V[irgini]a" (quoted in Freeman 1915: 275). The poor performance of the Confederate horsemen at Tom's Brook is evidence that these difficulties were not being overcome. Conditions continued to deteriorate during the ensuing winter and the last desperate Confederate cavalry charge was made at Appomattox Court House on April 9, 1865.

ORDERS OF BATTLE

Lewis Ford, August 30, 1862

Confederate

Robertson's Brigade, Cavalry Division, Army of Northern Virginia (Brig Gen Beverly H. Robertson). Brigade casualties: KIA 18; WIA 78; MIA 18 = 114. 2nd Virginia Cavalry (Col Thomas T. Munford (WIA)); 6th Virginia Cavalry (Col Thomas S. Flournoy); 7th Virginia Cavalry (Capt Samuel B. Myers); 12th Virginia Cavalry (Col A.W. Harman).

Union

Cavalry Brigade, II Corps, Army of Virginia (Brig Gen John Buford). Brigade casualties: KIA 15, WIA 35, MIA 150 = 200. 1st Michigan Cavalry (Col Thornton F. Brodhead (DOW), Maj Charles Town (WIA)); 1st West Virginia Cavalry (Lt Col Nathaniel P. Richmond); 1st Vermont Cavalry (Col Charles H. Tompkins); 5th New York Cavalry (First Ira Harris Guard) (Col Othniel De Forest); 4th New York Cavalry (First Regiment, German Cavalry).

Cavalry Brigade, I Corps, Army of Virginia (unofficially attached) (Lt Col Ferries Nazer)

Buckland Mills, October 19, 1863

Confederate

Cavalry Corps, Army of Northern Virginia (Maj Gen James E.B. Stuart)

Hampton's Division (Maj Gen James E.B. Stuart)
Gordon's Brigade (Brig Gen James B. Gordon): 1st North Carolina Cavalry (9th Regiment, NCST) (Lt Col Rufus Barringer); 2nd North Carolina Cavalry (19th Regiment, NCST) (Col William G. Robinson); 4th North Carolina Cavalry (41st Regiment, NCST) (Lt Col Edward Cantwell); 5th North Carolina Cavalry (63rd Regiment, NCST) (Lt Col James H. McNeill).
Jones'/Rosser's Brigade (Col Oliver Funsten): 7th Virginia Cavalry (Col Richard Dulany); 11th Virginia Cavalry (Lt Col Mottrom D. Ball); 12th Virginia Cavalry (Col Asher Harman).
Young's Brigade (Brig Gen Pierce M.B. Young): Cobb's (Georgia) Legion (Lt Col Barrington S. King); Jeff Davis (Mississippi) Legion (Lt Col J.F. Waring); Phillip's (Georgia) Legion (Lt Col W.G. Delony).

Fitzhugh Lee's Division
W.H.F. Lee's Brigade (Col John R. Chambliss, Jr.): 9th Virginia Cavalry (Lt Col Thomas Waller); 10th Virginia Cavalry (Col J. Lucius Davis); 13th Virginia Cavalry (Col Jefferson Phillips).
Wickham's Brigade (Col Thomas H. Owen): 1st Virginia Cavalry (Col Richard Carter); 2nd Virginia Cavalry (Col Thomas Munford); 3rd Virginia Cavalry (not known); 4th Virginia Cavalry (Col William F.H. Payne).

Lomax's Brigade (Brig Gen Lunsford L. Lomax): 1st Maryland Battalion Cavalry (Lt Col Ridgley Brown); 5th Virginia Cavalry (Col Reuben Boston); 6th Virginia Cavalry (Lt Col John Shackleford Green); 15th Virginia Cavalry (Maj C.R. Collins).

Beckham's Battalion Artillery (Maj R.F. Beckham) Breathed's (Virginia) Battery (Stuart Horse Artillery, 1st Battery) (Capt J. Breathed); Chew's (Virginia) Battery (Ashby Horse Artillery) (Capt R.P. Chew); Griffin's (Maryland) Battery (2nd Maryland Artillery Company) (Capt W.H. Griffin); Hart's (South Carolina) Battery (Washington Light Artillery) (Capt James F. Hart); McGregor's (Virginia) Battery (Stuart Horse Artillery, 2nd Battery) (Capt W.M. McGregor); Moorman's (Virginia) Battery (Lynchburg Horse Artillery) (Capt. M. N. Moorman).

Union

Third Division, Cavalry Corps, Army of the Potomac (Brig Gen Hugh Judson Kilpatrick)
Headquarters Guard: 1st Ohio Cavalry, Companies A and C.
1st Brigade (Brig Gen Henry E. Davies, Jr.): 2nd New York Cavalry (Harris Light Cavalry) (Lt Col Otto Harhaus); 5th New York Cavalry (Maj John Hammond); 18th Pennsylvania Cavalry (Maj Harvey B. Van Vorhis); 1st West Virginia Cavalry (AKA 1st Virginia Cavalry, US Volunteers) (Maj Charles E. Capehart).
2nd Brigade (Brig Gen George A. Custer): 1st Michigan Cavalry (Col Charles H. Town); 5th Michigan Cavalry (Col Russell A. Alger); 6th Michigan Cavalry (Lt Col Henry E. Thompson); 7th Michigan Cavalry (Col William D. Mann); 1st Vermont Cavalry (Col Edward B. Sawyer).
1st Brigade Horse Artillery (attached to Third Division) Battery M, 2nd US Artillery (1/Lt Alexander C.M. Pennington, Jr.); Battery E, 4th US Artillery (Capt Samuel Elder).

1st North Carolina Cavalry (9th Regiment, NCST)

Lt Col Rufus Barringer (WIA), Maj William H.H. Cowles plus one adjutant (ranked first lieutenant), one assistant commissary of subsistence (ranked captain), one assistant surgeon, one quartermaster sergeant, one commissary sergeant, one ordnance sergeant, one hospital steward, one chief bugler, one second bugler, one "staff blacksmith," and 23 company-grade officer and 568 men = 591 all ranks. (NB: numbers approx as listed "present or accounted for.") Casualties: 1 KIA, 4 WIA = 5.

Co. A: Capt John L. Smith, 1/Lt David W. Eller plus 70 men.
Co. B: 1/Lt Whitmel Hill Anthony plus 94 men.
Co. C (Mecklenburg Rangers): Capt Marcus D.L. McLeod, 2/Lt James L. Morrow, 3/Lt William B. Field plus 71 men.
Co. D (Watauga Rangers): Capt John C. Blair, 2/Lt Daniel P. Mast plus 64 men.
Co. E: Capt Cadwallader Jones Iredell, 1/Lt Jerome H. Fuller, 2/Lt William Jones White plus 54 men.
Co. F: 1/Lt Noah P. Foard plus 60 men. William A. Blackwelder wounded at Buckland.

Co. G (Buncombe Rangers): 1/Lt Henry S. Coleman, 2/Lt Thomas L. Matthias plus 59 men.
Co. H: Capt James Cole Borden, 1/Lt Benjamin T. Person, 3/Lt John H. Hayes plus 38 men.
Co. I: Capt Wiley Alexander Barrier, 1/Lt Kerr Craige, 2/Lt William G. Grady (KIA) plus 64 men. Timothy Merritt wounded in right thigh. George Washington Miller WIA.
Co. K: Capt William M. Addington, 1/Lt Samuel Beniah Gibson, 2/Lt Jacob M. Gillespie plus 58 men. Silas Tuthero WIA.

2nd New York Cavalry (Harris Light Cavalry)
Lt Col Otto Harhaus, Maj John E. Naylor, Maj Edwin F. Cook plus eight staff consisting of two adjutants, one commissary of subsistence (ranked sergeant), one regimental commissary sergeant, one acting bandmaster, one regimental sergeant major, one regimental quartermaster sergeant, one regimental saddler sergeant (POW), and 23 company-grade officer and 641 man = 652 all ranks. Casualties: 4 KIA, 3 WIA, 1 MIA, 43 POW = 51.

Co. A: Capt Lucian H. Southard, 1/Lt Robert Loudon, plus 80 men. Casualties: 5 POW = 5.
Co. B: 1/Lt Charles E. Morton, plus 52 men. Casualties: 5 POW = 5.
Co. C: Capt John F. Mitchell, 1/Lt Edward W. Whittaker, plus 57 men. Casualties: 5 POW = 5.
Co. D: Capt Marcus Coon, 1/Lt Albert Wilson, 2/Lt Andrew S. Glover, plus 50 men. Casualties: 4 POW = 4.
Co. E: 1/Lt Frederick C. Lord, 2/Lt Willard W. Glazier, plus 47 men. Casualties: 5 POW = 5.
Co. F: Sgt Jeremiah Ostrander plus 46 men. Casualties: 2 POW = 2.
Co. G: Capt Henry Grinton, plus 54 men. Casualties: 5 POW, 1 WIA, 1 MIA = 7.
Co. H: Capt Frederick Poughkeepsie, 2/Lt Martin F. Hatch, plus 38 men. Casualties: 2 POW = 2.
Co. I: 1/Lt Charles D. Carlton, 2/Lt Perry Homan, plus 58 men. Casualties: 3 KIA, 2 POW = 5.
Co. K: 1/Lt William R. Mattison, plus 47 men. Casualties: 1 WIA, 4 POW = 5.
Co. L: Capt Thomas B. Moore, 1/Lt Francis M. Plum, 2/Lt William B. Shafer, plus 65 men. Casualties: 1 KIA, 1 WIA, 4 POW = 6.
Co. M: 1/Lt Seymour L. Burroughs plus 47 men. No casualties.

Tom's Brook, October 9, 1864

Confederate
II Corps (Lt Gen Jubal A. Early), Cavalry

Lomax's Division (Maj Gen Lunsford L. Lomax)
Johnson's Brigade (Brig Gen Bradley T. Johnson): 8th Virginia Cavalry (Col James M. Corns); 21st Virginia Cavalry (Col W.E. Peters); 34th Virginia Battalion (Lt Col Vinson A. Witcher); 36th Virginia Battalion (Maj James W. Sweeney).
Jackson's Brigade (Brig Gen H.B. Davidson): 1st Maryland Cavalry (Lt Col Gustavus Dorsey); 19th Virginia Cavalry (Col William L. Jackson); 20th Virginia Cavalry (Col W.W. Arnett);

46th Virginia Battalion (Maj Henry D. Ruffner); 47th Virginia Battalion (Capt Elias M. Walker).
Artillery: Capt John J. Shoemaker's Virginia Horse Artillery.
Rosser's (Fitzhugh Lee's) Division (Brig Gen Thomas L. Rosser)
Wickham's Brigade (Col Thomas T. Munford): 1st Virginia Cavalry (Col Richard W. Carter); 2nd Virginia Cavalry (Maj Cary Breckenridge); 3rd Virginia Cavalry (Col Thomas H. Owen); 4th Virginia Cavalry (Lt Col William B. Wooldridge).
Rosser's (Laurel) Brigade (Col Richard H. Dulany (WIA); Col Oliver Funsten): 7th Virginia Cavalry (Lt Col Thomas Marshall); 11th Virginia Cavalry (Maj Edward H. McDonald); 12th Virginia Cavalry (Capt Emanuel Sipe (poss. WIA)); 35th Virginia Battalion (1/Lt Nicholas Dorsey).
Payne's Brigade (Brig Gen William H.F. Payne): 5th Virginia Cavalry (Col Reuben B. Boston); 6th Virginia Cavalry (Lt Col Daniel T. Richards); 15th Virginia Cavalry (Col William B. Ball).
Artillery: Capt William "Tuck" Carter's Virginia Light Artillery, Thomson's Artillery Battalion.

Union
Middle Military Division (Maj Gen Philip Sheridan)

Cavalry, Provisional Division, Army of West Virginia (Brig Gen Alfred T. A. Torbert). Escort: 1st Rhode Island Cavalry (Maj William H. Turner, Jr.)

First Division (Brig Gen Wesley Merritt)
1st Brigade (Col James H. Kidd): 1st Michigan Cavalry (Capt Andrew W. Duggan); 5th Michigan Cavalry (Maj Smith H. Hastings); 6th Michigan Cavalry (Maj Charles W. Deane); 7th Michigan Cavalry (Maj Daniel H. Darling); 6th New York Battery (Capt Joseph W. Martin).
2nd Brigade (Col Thomas C. Devin): 4th New York Cavalry (Maj Edward Schwartz); 6th New York Cavalry (Capt George E. Farmer); 9th New York Cavalry (Col George S. Nichols); 19th New York Cavalry (1st Dragoons) (Col Alfred Gibbs); Batteries K and L, 1st US Artillery (1/Lt Franck E. Taylor).
Reserve Brigade (Col Charles R. Lowell, Jr.): 2nd Massachusetts Cavalry (Lt Col Casper Crowninshield); 1st US Cavalry (Capt Eugene M. Baker); 2nd US Cavalry (Capt Robert S. Smith; 5th US Cavalry (1/Lt Gustavus Urban).

Third Division (Brig Gen George A. Custer)
1st Brigade (Col Alexander C.M. Pennington, Jr.): 1st Connecticut Cavalry (Capt Edwin W. French); 3rd New Jersey Cavalry (Lt Col Charles C. Suydam); 2nd New York Cavalry (Capt Andrew S. Glover); 5th New York Cavalry (Maj Abram H. Krom); 2nd Ohio Cavalry (Lt Col George A. Purington); 18th Pennsylvania Cavalry (Maj John W. Phillips).
2nd Brigade (Col William Wells): 3rd Indiana Cavalry (two companies) (1/Lt Benjamin F. Gilbert); 1st New Hampshire Cavalry (battalion) (Col John L. Thompson); 8th New York Cavalry (Rochester Regiment) (Lt Col William H. Benjamin); 22nd New York Cavalry (Maj Charles C. Brown); 1st Vermont Cavalry (Lt Col John W. Bennett);: Companies B and L, 2nd US Horse Artillery (Capt Charles H. Peirce); Companies C, F, and K, 3rd US Horse Artillery (Capt Dunbar R. Ransom).

SELECT BIBLIOGRAPHY

Beale, Richard L.T. (1899). *History of the Ninth Virginia Cavalry in the War Between the States*. Richmond, VA: B.F. Johnson Publishing Company.

Blackford, Lt Col W.W. (1945). *War Years with Jeb Stuart*. New York, NY: Charles Scribner's Sons.

Boudrye, Rev. L.N. (1868). *Historic Records of the Fifth New York Cavalry, First Ira Harris Guard*. Albany, NY: J. Munsell.

Clark, Walter, ed. (1901). *Histories of the Several Regiments and Battalions in the Great War 1861–'65*. Raleigh, NC: published by the State.

Confederate States of America, Adjutant and Inspector General (1861). *Uniform and Dress of the Army of the Confederate States*. Richmond, VA: Charles H. Wynne, Printer.

Cooke, Gen Philip St. George (1861). *Cavalry Tactics, or, Regulations for the instruction, formations, and movements of the cavalry of the army and volunteers of the United States*, two volumes. Washington, DC: Government Printing Office.

Crouch, Howard R. (2003). *Horse Equipment of the Civil War Era*. Fairfax, VA: SCS Publications.

Denison, Lt Col George T. (1868). *Modern Cavalry: Its Organisation, Armament and Employment in War*. London: Thomas Bosworth.

Driver, Robert J, Jr. (1991). *1st Virginia Cavalry*. Virginia Regimental Histories Series. Lynchburg, VA: H.E. Howard, Inc.

Driver, Robert J, Jr., & H.E. Howard (1995). *2nd Virginia Cavalry*. Virginia Regimental Histories Series. Lynchburg, VA: H.E. Howard, Inc.

Fay, J.B. (1915). "Cavalry Fight at Second Manassas," *Confederate Veteran*, Vol. 23: 263–64.

Fonzo, Stephen (2008). *A Documentary and Landscape Analysis of the Buckland Mills Battlefield* (VA042). Gainesville, VA: Buckland Preservation Society.

Freeman, Douglas Southall, ed. (1915). *Lee's Dispatches: Unpublished Letters of Robert E. Lee, C.S.A.* New York, NY & London: G.P. Putnam's Sons.

Frye, Dennis E. (1988). *12th Virginia Cavalry*. "Virginia Regimental Histories Series." Lynchburg, VA: H.E. Howard, Inc.

Gallagher, Gary W., ed. (2006). *The Shenandoah Valley Campaign of 1864*. Chapel Hill, NC: University of North Carolina Press.

Gerleman, David J. "Warhorse! Union Cavalry Mounts." *North and South Magazine* Vol. 2, No. 2 (January 1999): 47–61.

Glazier, Willard (1870). *Three Years in the Federal Cavalry*. New York, NY: R.H. Ferguson & Co.

Glazier, Willard (1875). *Battles for the Union*. Cincinnati, OH: Dustin, Gilman & Co.

Harrell, Roger H. (2004). *The 2nd North Carolina Cavalry*. Jefferson, NC: McFarland & Co., Inc.

Harris, Moses (1890). "With the Reserve Brigade," *Journal of the United States Cavalry Association*, 3.

Hennessy, John J. (1999). *Return to Bull Run: The Campaign and Battle of Second Manassas*. Norman, OK: Oklahoma University Press.

Hillard, George Stillman (1865). *Life and Campaigns of George B. McClellan, Major-general U.S. Army*. Philadelphia, PA: J.B. Lippincott.

Howell, Edgar H. (1982). *United States Army Headgear 1855–1902: Catalog of United States Army Uniforms in the Collection of the Smithsonian Institution*, Vol. II. Washington, DC: Smithsonian Institution.

Hundley, Gen George J. (1895). "Reminiscences of the First and Last Days of the War," *Southern Historical Society Papers*, Vol. 23: 294–313.

Hutton, Paul Andrew (1992). *The Custer Reader*. Lincoln, NE: University of Nebraska Press.

Johnson, L.E. (2007). *He Kept the Colors: The True Story of the General, the Old Man and the Flag*. Bloomington, IN: Author House.

Kesterson, Brian Stuart (1993). *The Last Survivor: The Memoirs of George William Watson – a Horse Soldier in the 12th Virginia Cavalry*. Washington, WV: Night Hawk Press.

Kidd, J.H. (1908). *Personal Recollections of a cavalryman with Custer's Michigan cavalry brigade in the Civil War*. Iona, MI: Sentinel Print Co.

Knopp, Ken R. (2001). *Confederate Saddles & Horse Equipment*. Orange, VA: Publisher's Press, Inc.

Krick, Robert (1982). 9th Virginia Cavalry. Virginia Regimental Histories Series. Lynchburg, VA: H.E. Howard, Inc.

Lee, William O., compiler (1902). *Personal and Historical Sketches of and by members of the Seventh Regiment Michigan Volunteer Cavalry 1862–1865*. Detroit, MI: Seventh Michigan Cavalry Association.

Longacre, Edward G. (1995). *General John Buford: A Military Biography*. Conshohocken, PA: Combined Publishing.

Longacre, Edward G. (2002). *Lee's Cavalrymen: A History of the Mounted Forces of the Army of Northern Virginia*. Mechanicsburg, PA: Stackpole Books.

Longacre, Edward G. (2000). *Lincoln's Cavalrymen: A History of the Mounted Forces of the Army of the Potomac*. Mechanicsburg, PA: Stackpole Books.

Longacre, Edward G. (1986). *The Cavalry at Gettysburg*. Lincoln, NE: University of Nebraska Press.

Lowe, David W. (1992). *Study of Civil War Sites in the Shenandoah Valley of Virginia*. US Department of the Interior: National Park Service.

McAulay, John D. (1996). *Carbines of the U.S. Cavalry 1861–1905*. Lincoln, RI: Andrew Mowbray Inc.

McDonald, William N. (2002). *A History of the Laurel Brigade. Originally the Ashby Cavalry of the Army of Northern Virginia and Chew's Battery*. Baltimore, MD: The John Hopkins University Press.

Meyer, Henry C. (1911). *Civil War Experiences Under Bayard, Gregg, Kilpatrick, Custer, Raulston, and Newberry, 1862, 1863, 1864*. New York, NY: G.P. Putnam & Sons.

Moyer, H.P. (1911). *History of the Seventeenth Regiment Pennsylvania Cavalry*. Lebanon, PA: Sowers Printing Co.

Munford, Thomas T. (1884–85). "Reminiscences of the Cavalry Operations: Operations Under Rosser," *Southern Historical Society Papers*, Vol. 12, 342–50 & Vol. 13, 133–44.

Myers, Frank M. (1871). *The Comanches: A History of White's Battalion, Virginia Cavalry*. Baltimore, MD: Kelly, Piet & Co.

Nanzig, Thomas P., ed. (2007). *The Civil War Memoirs of a Virginia Cavalryman: Lt. Robert T. Hubard, Jr.* Tuscaloosa, AL: University of Alabama Press.

Neese, George M. (1911). *Three Years in the Confederate Horse Artillery*. New York, NY & Washington, DC: The Neale Publishing Co.

Norton, Henry, ed. (1889). *Deeds of Daring, or the Eighth N.Y. Volunteer Cavalry*. Norwich, NY: Chenango Telegraph Printing House.

Publication Committee (1909). *History of the Eighteenth Regiment of Cavalry, Pennsylvania Volunteers (163rd Regiment of the Line)*. New York, NY: Publication Committee of the Regimental Association.

Robertson, John (1882). *Michigan in the War*. Lansing, MI: W.S. George & Co.

Sheridan, Philip H. (1888). *Personal Memoirs of P.H. Sheridan*. 2 vols. New York, NY: Charles L. Webster & Co.

Scott, Robert N. (1880–1901). *Official Records of the War of the Rebellion*. Washington, DC: Government Printing Office. Referred to as *OR* followed by series, volume, part, and page numbers.

Scott, Maj Gen Winfield (1834). *A System of Tactics; or, Rules for the exercises and manoeuvres of the Cavalry and Light Infantry and Riflemen of the United States*. Washington, DC: F.P. Blair.

Starr, Stephen Z. (1981). *The Union Cavalry in the Civil War. Vol. 1: From Fort Sumter to Gettysburg 1861–1863*. Baton Rouge, LA: Louisiana State University Press.

Starr, Stephen Z. (1981). *The Union Cavalry in the Civil War. Vol. 2: The War in the East from Gettysburg to Appomattox 1863–1865*. Baton Rouge, LA: Louisiana State University Press.

Stiles, Kenneth L. (1985). *4th Virginia Cavalry*. Virginia Regimental Histories Series. Lynchburg, VA: H.E. Howard, Inc.

Tenney, Frances Andrews (1914). *War Diary of Luman Harris Tenney 1861–1865*. Cleveland, OH: Evangelical Publishing House.

Urwin, J.W. Gregory (1983). *Custer Victorious: The Civil War Battles of General George Armstrong Custer*. Rutherford, NJ: Combined University Presses.

US War Department (1855). *Cavalry Tactics*, three parts. Philadelphia, PA: Lippincott, Grambo, & Co.

Vandiver, Frank E. (1947). *Confederate Blockade Running Through Bermuda, 1861–1865, Letters and Cargo Manifests*. Austin, TX: University of Texas Press.

Wert, Jeffry D. (2008). *Cavalrymen of the Lost Cause: A Biography of J.E.B. Stuart*. New York, NY: Simon & Schuster.

Wittenberg, Eric J. (1995). "The Battle of Tom's Brook, October 9, 1864," *North and South Trader's Civil War*, Vol. 10, No. 1, 30–45.

Wittenberg, Eric J. (2010). *The Battle of Brandy Station: North America's Largest Cavalry Battle*. Charleston, SC: The History Press.

Manuscripts

"A bill to increase the efficiency of the cavalry of the Confederate States." Proposed January 2, 1865. Cf. Journal/Confederate States America. Congress Parrish & Willingham. Confederate imprints.

Anthony, Whit. (n.d.). "Cavalry Fight at Bucklands, Virginia, October 19, 1863." Typescript in the Smith Papers, Southern Historical Association, University of North Carolina at Chapel Hill.

Alfred G. Ryder diary, Michigan Historical Collection, Bentley Historical Library, University of Michigan, Ann Arbor, MI: entry of August 29, 1862.

Civil War Miscellaneous Collection, US Army Military History Institute, Carlisle, PA: William Porter Wilkin to Dear Wife, September 7, 1862.

Confederate Adjutant and Inspector General's Department, Inspection Reports and Related Records, US National Archives, Washington, DC. Col Walter H. Jenifer to Acting Assistant Inspector General Col B.H. Shelton, October 18, 1864.

Jedediah Hotchkiss Papers, Library of Congress: A.W. Harman to Jedediah Hotchkiss, March 15, 1886.

Letters of William H. Emslie, Co. G, 2nd New York Cavalry. http://localhistory.morrisville.edu/sites/letters/emslie1.html (accessed October 6, 2014).

Order Book, Cavalry Corps, Army of the Potomac, Civil War Miscellaneous Collection, US Army Military History Institute, Carlisle, PA: John Buford to Maj Gen Alfred Pleasonton, September 16, 1863.

University of Virginia, Beverly Kennon Whittle Papers.

Virginia Historical Society, Richmond, Virginia: J.E.B. Stuart Papers, Maj Gen J.E.B. Stuart to My Darling One, September 4, 1862.

Newspapers

Charlotte Observer, Charlotte, NC (*CO*); *Charleston Daily Courier*, SC (*CDC*); *Charleston Mercury*, SC (*CM*); *Columbus Daily Enquirer*, GA (*CDE*); *Detroit Free Press*, IL (*DFP*); *Omaha World Herald*, NEB (*OWH*); *National Tribune*, Washington, DC (*NT*); *New York Commercial Advertiser* (*NYCA*); *New-York Tribune* (*NYT*); *Lowell Daily Citizen & News*, MA (*LDCN*); *New York Daily Reformer*, Watertown, NY (*NYDR*); *Philadelphia Inquirer*, PA (*PI*); *Plain Dealer*, Cleveland, OH (*PD*); *Richmond Examiner*, VA (*RE*); *St. Albans Daily Messenger*, VT (*SADM*).

INDEX

Figures in **bold** refer to illustrations.